AUTHORITY FROM GOD

How and why you can kick the Devil out of your life

RANDY CLARK

ACKNOWLEDGMENTS

Thank you to Karen, my wife of 28 years, for your help in putting this book together. Your editing skills and input were invaluable in preparing the manuscript for publication. And thank you for your ongoing encouragement and belief in me. Together, we continue to pursue God's dream for our lives.

Thank you to Billy Joe Daugherty, Pastor of Victory Christian Center in Tulsa, Oklahoma. Your willingness to follow the vision God put in your heart concerning Victory Bible Institute created a wonderful opportunity for me to begin a lifelong process of studying and teaching the word of God.

Thank you to Dr. Ronald E. Cottle for birthing Christian Life School of Theology, now Beacon Institute of Ministry, and allowing me to teach the course described in this book in churches all across America.

INTRODUCTION

"If you know the enemy and know yourself, you need not fear the results of a hundred battles. If you know neither the enemy nor yourself, you will succumb in every battle."
- Sun Tzu: "On The Art Of War" ca. 500 BC.

I first began to hear the truths described in this book while attending Bible School in 1979. In 1984, I was given the opportunity to teach a course on "The Believer's Authority" at Victory Bible Institute in Tulsa, Oklahoma. I immediately began to immerse myself in the subject. I read books on the topic and related topics from numerous authors. I studied the Bible intensely. Soon, God began to give me a revelation and a path to take for this course. I have since taught this course in numerous Bible schools in the United States and other countries. The teaching has been refined and focused many times. This book is a result of years of study and presentation of the awesome truth about the authority given to believers.

I believe the Bible is God's revelation to us. You will find extensive use of Scriptures throughout this book. I believe it is important that you see what God has to say about this subject. That is why I chose to print out most Scriptures rather than simply give a reference. I also frequently underlined portions of Scripture quotations to help in understanding particular truths. In addition, I used several different modern translations of the Bible to provide a more complete revelation of God's thoughts.

Perspective is an important consideration when approaching any truth from the Bible. People can look at the same truth and see different aspects. It is like climbing a mountain. A climbing team that climbs the north side of a mountain would describe the mountain one way. A team that ascends the south side would describe an entirely different point of view. It is the same mountain, but two different viewpoints. You don't really know all about the mountain until you hear from people who have climbed it from all angles.

I encourage you to keep the concept of perspective in mind. This book describes certain aspects of the truth of the believer's authority. Another minister may have a different view of the same subject. Don't throw my book out because it is somewhat different than what you hear someone else teach. Don't discard someone else's description because it differs from mine. The only way you will get a full understanding of the topic is to add all the revelation together. No one person has all the answers. We each have part of the truth. One book cannot cover every possible angle on the subject.

Jesus paid a high price to set us free from the penalty of sin and control of Satan. My prayer is that the Holy Spirit will impart to you a fresh understanding of this incredible miracle Jesus provided to us.

CONTENTS

CHAPTER 1

CREATION AND CHAOS

The majesty of the original creation was more than the human mind can fathom. The glory of God provided a brilliant light that penetrated into every part of this vast universe. There were no shadows. Heaven and Earth were in perfect order. The angels were divided into groups with specific functions. Some of them simply cried, "Holy, holy, holy" around the throne of Almighty God. One angel stood out from the others. He was the most beautiful creature God had created. All the other angels reported to this angel. His name was Lucifer.

Lucifer had it all. He served as God's most trusted created being. Lucifer had unlimited access to God at all times. Lucifer had a throne from which he ruled over all of God's original creation. His body was a musical instrument which he used to praise his Creator. Lucifer could have served in his position of authority and beauty for all of eternity. But he didn't. Lucifer chose to rebel against God. Being number two in the universe wasn't good enough.

Lucifer committed the first sin and thereby altered the course of history forever. His rebellion caused God's original creation to be destroyed. Lucifer's name became Satan. His beauty and wisdom became corrupted because of sin. Satan's rebellion against God continued into the second version of the Earth which God put together. He attacked God's new rulers on this planet. He infected mankind with the plague of sin. It looked as if Satan had won. God's creation was corrupted once again.

But God had a plan. God's plan would put an end to Satan's rebellious influence. God's plan would restore mankind to a position of authority over Satan. God's plan was simple and complex at the same time. Satan could not figure it out. But you can understand it if you will go with me on this incredible journey into the word of God to understand the magnificent message of the believer's authority.

THE BEGINNING

We will start our journey in the book of beginnings, the Old Testament book of Genesis.

In the beginning God created the heavens and the earth. (Genesis 1:1)

When was the beginning? The beginning does not refer to the beginning of God because He does not have a beginning. God <u>has</u> always existed and always <u>will</u> exist. It is hard for our human minds to imagine something that has no beginning or end. The beginning refers to when God created the Heavens and the Earth. So how long ago was that? If we use the recorded history of the Bible and other sources, we can calculate that Adam, the first created human being, began his existence approximately 6,000 years ago. But this verse does not mention creating Adam. It just talks about creating the Heavens and the Earth. This beginning could have been millions of years ago. Many scientists say the Earth is millions of years old. Maybe they are right. Their opinion does not contradict the Bible because the Bible does not say when God created the Heavens and the Earth. We find something very interesting, however, in the next verse.

The earth was without form, and void; and darkness was on the face of the deep. And the Spirit of God was hovering over the face of the waters. (Genesis 1:2)

In order to understand what is described here we will have to examine the original Hebrew text. Don't be alarmed. I will not bore you with a Hebrew language lesson. If you stay with me for just a short time, you will understand an amazing event in the history of the world.

The Hebrew word translated "was" as in *"The earth was without form..."* is from the Hebrew "hayah." This is a verb which means "to become." This Hebrew word is translated elsewhere in the Bible as "became, came and come to pass." This makes a big difference. Saying *"The earth was without form..."* implies that God made it that way. Using a literal interpretation of the original Hebrew text, *"The earth became without form..."* makes it clear that the Earth as God **originally** created it was not without form and void.

The words translated *"without form"* are from the Hebrew "tohuw" which means "waste, desolation or confusion." This Hebrew word is translated elsewhere in the Bible as "waste, vain, confusion, empty, vanity, nothing and wilderness."

The word translated *"void"* is from the Hebrew "bohuw" which means "empty, ruin or void."

When we put these definitions together, the Scripture reads like this, **"And the Earth became a desolate wasteland, empty, without form and covered with darkness."** Since the Earth became a desolate wasteland, something must have happened to cause it to change from its original condition to a desolate, ruined condition of confusion and darkness. The Bible says in *1 Corinthians 14:33, "For God is not the author of confusion but of peace, as in all the churches of the saints."* God obviously did not create a confused Earth. Does it make sense for God to create a mess and then clean it up?

> *For thus says the LORD, Who created the heavens, Who is God, Who formed the earth and made it, Who has established it, Who did not create it in vain, Who formed it to be inhabited: "I am the LORD, and there is no other. (Isaiah 45:18)*

Notice the Scripture above says God did not create the Earth **"in vain."** The Hebrew word translated "vain" is "tohuw," the same word translated "without form" in *Genesis 1:2*. God did not create the Earth "vain, without form or desolate." He created the Earth to be inhabited, capable of sustaining life. The Earth was in no condition to be inhabited the way it was described in *Genesis 1:2*. Since God did not create it as a desolate wasteland, what happened to cause it to become that way?

LUCIFER'S ORIGIN AND FALL

The answer to the question is found by examining Lucifer's relationship with God. Two passages of Old Testament Scriptures provide great insight into Lucifer's original condition and his monumental mistake. To understand these passages you have to understand the Biblical interpretation principle called "the law of double reference." This principle is demonstrated when a visible person is addressed while at the same time a spirit who controls that person is also addressed. A New Testament example of this principle is found when Jesus began to tell His disciples He had to go to Jerusalem. Jesus described the horrible things that would happen to Him there. He told how He would suffer at the hands of the religious leaders and be killed. Peter took Jesus aside and rebuked Him, saying that those things would not happen. This is how Jesus responded.

> *But He turned and said to Peter, "Get behind Me, Satan! You are an offense to Me, for you are not mindful of the things of God, but the things of men." (Matthew 16:23)*

Jesus turned and spoke to "Peter." But then He addressed "Satan." Did Peter turn into Satan? No. Jesus looked at Peter, but He spoke to the spirit who had inspired Peter to speak those words. Satan had influenced Peter to rebuke Jesus. The same principle is found in Ezekiel 28, the first Scripture where we find a description of Lucifer.

> *The word of the LORD came to me again, saying, "Son of man, say to the prince of Tyre, 'Thus says*

the Lord GOD: "Because your heart is lifted up, And you say, 'I am a god, I sit in the seat of gods, In the midst of the seas,' Yet you are a man, and not a god, Though you set your heart as the heart of a god (Ezekiel 28:1-2)

Ezekiel prophesied to the "prince" of the city of Tyre. He used the Hebrew word, "nagid," which means "ruler." In verses 1-10, Ezekiel describes how the ruler of Tyre is full of pride concerning his wisdom and accomplishments. He rebukes this ruler because his pride has gone to the extreme of calling himself a god. Then in verse 12 the prophet begins to address the spirit who is controlling the ruler of Tyre.

Moreover the word of the LORD came to me, saying, "Son of man, take up a lamentation for the king of Tyre, and say to him, ...(Ezekiel 28:11-12)

Now he speaks to the "king" (Hebrew, "melek") of Tyre, instead of the "ruler or prince." He talks to the spirit who is controlling the ruler of the city. He began by talking to the human "prince" of Tyre and then begins to talk to the satanic "king" of Tyre who is actually in control. It is clear from the description in the following verses this can only be Satan in his original created condition when he was known as Lucifer.

...'Thus says the Lord GOD: "You were the seal of perfection, Full of wisdom and perfect in beauty. (Ezekiel 28:12)

God created a perfect Lucifer with no flaws. He wasn't unfinished or incomplete. He was full of the wisdom of Almighty God. He had a complete understanding of everything he was required to know. Lucifer was the most gorgeous creature in God's vast universe.

You were in Eden, the garden of God;... (Ezekiel 28:13)

This may refer to his entrance into the Garden of Eden to tempt Adam and Eve after the Earth had been restored. It most likely, however, refers to an earlier Eden which existed in God's original creation. Satan did not look like he is described in the rest of this verse when he was in the Garden of Eden with Adam and Eve.

> *... Every precious stone was your covering: The sardius, topaz, and diamond, Beryl, onyx, and jasper, Sapphire, turquoise, and emerald with gold... (Ezekiel 28:13)*

Can you imagine how resplendent Lucifer looked? He was covered with these magnificent stones. He looked more stunning than anything we have seen in this life. I am sure he attracted a lot of attention wherever he went. No wonder the previous verse said he was "perfect in beauty."

> *...The workmanship of your timbrels and pipes was prepared for you on the day you were created. (Ezekiel 28:13)*

What are timbrels and pipes used for? They are used to make music. Lucifer's body was capable of producing music. He did not have to learn how to play a musical instrument. His body was already a musical instrument. He had all this beauty and musical ability from the day he was created.

> *"You were the anointed cherub who covers; I established you; You were on the holy mountain of God; You walked back and forth in the midst of fiery stones. (Ezekiel 28:14)*

A cherub is an angel. From other Scriptures we know that cherubs protect the throne of God. Lucifer was an angel who had a special anointing from God. He had been anointed, or enabled, by God to function in a certain area of authority. Lucifer did not work his way up to this position. God established him in his position when he was created. In his position of great authority, Lucifer also had unlimited access to God in what is called "the holy mountain of God." He was able to walk back and forth in the fiery presence of God.

> *You were perfect in your ways from the day you were created, Till iniquity was found in you. (Ezekiel 28:15)*

Lucifer started out right. He was not corrupt from the beginning. Notice he is a created being. He had a beginning. Satan is not just a symbol of evil. He was created by God and he was perfect in his original condition. But something terrible happened. Iniquity was found in him. Iniquity was not put in him by God. It was self-generated. This is one of the greatest mysteries of all time. How could Lucifer decide to sin when he was created perfect, full of the wisdom of God and with perfect access to God? It is a question for which I have no answer. I just know it happened.

> *"By the abundance of your trading You became filled with violence within, And you sinned; Therefore I cast you as a profane thing Out of the mountain of God; And I destroyed you, O covering cherub, From the midst of the fiery stones. "Your heart was lifted up because of your beauty; You corrupted your wisdom for the sake of your splendor; I cast you to the ground, I laid you before kings, That they might gaze at you. (Ezekiel 28:16-17)*

The word translated "trading" carries the connotation of traveling and conducting business transactions such as a peddler or traveling merchant. When a merchant conducts business, something passes through his hands. Money from the customer comes in and merchandise goes out. Part of Lucifer's responsibility as a "guardian angel" or "cherub," was to deliver God's commands to the creation and deliver the praise of the creation back to God. Those things passed through Lucifer's hands. All the praise from His creation obviously belonged to God. But Lucifer apparently decided to siphon off some of the praise for himself. After all, wasn't he the most beautiful creation in Heaven and Earth? Wasn't he wiser than any other created being? Surely a little bit of praise belonged to him. Maybe a lot of praise belonged to him.

A modern-day example would work like this. John is the manager of a discount store. Every day he is responsible for taking the receipts from the store to the bank. He does not deposit the money in his own account. He deposits the money in the discount store account. He does this for several years. Every day the money passes through his hands into the business account. But one day he begins to think a new thought.

"I am a great manager. I have been working here for a long time. They make a lot of money because of me. I deserve a little bit of this deposit."

John reaches into the bag on the way to the bank and takes out $1,000. What is wrong with this picture? The money did not belong to John. It was supposed to pass through his hands to the rightful owner. But John decided to keep some money that did not belong to him.

This is what Lucifer did. The praise which belonged to God alone passed through Lucifer for many years. He passed it all on to God just like he should have. But one day he thought a new thought.

"I am great. I deserve some of this praise."

Iniquity was found in Lucifer's heart. His will was no longer aligned with God's will. He tried to keep something that did not belong to him and he sinned. He plotted a violent overthrow of Heaven. But God won that battle and cast Lucifer out of His presence. Lucifer's authority and beauty were destroyed. He had corrupted himself by the decision he made. He refused to recognize the One Who had given him his wisdom and beauty.

> *"You defiled your sanctuaries By the multitude of your iniquities, By the iniquity of your trading; Therefore I brought fire from your midst; It devoured you, And I turned you to ashes upon the Earth In the sight of all who saw you. (Ezekiel 28:18)*

The Hebrew word translated "sanctuaries" in this Scripture means "a consecrated place, especially a palace, sanctuary or asylum." Who lives in a palace? One who rules lives in a palace. Lucifer defiled his place of authority by perverting the transfer of praise which belonged to God. The phrases referring to "fire" and "ashes" are used in other places in the Bible and are always figurative and not literal. Lucifer was not annihilated, but his original condition and authority were totally destroyed, and he was changed.

Isaiah was another prophet of God who provides us with insight into Lucifer's fall from perfection.

> *"How you are fallen from heaven, O Lucifer, son of the morning! How you are cut down to the ground, You who weakened the nations! For you have said in your heart: 'I will ascend into heaven, I will exalt my throne above the stars of God; I will also sit on the mount of the congregation On the farthest sides of the north; I will ascend above the heights of the clouds, I will be like the Most High.' (Isaiah 14:12-14)*

Lucifer fell from his Heavenly position because of pride. He was full of himself. Look at the five "I's" that cost Lucifer his throne: I will ascend into Heaven, I will exalt my throne, I will sit on the mount, I will ascend above the clouds, I will be like the Most High. God's will was no longer relevant to Lucifer. The only thing that mattered was what Lucifer wanted. He decided he wanted to be equal with God. How could he be so stupid? How can anyone think he can be "like the Most High?" Since God is the "Most High," how could anyone equal that? Somehow Lucifer decided he could do anything God could do.

> *Yet you shall be brought down to Sheol, To the lowest depths of the Pit. "Those who see you will gaze at you, And consider you, saying: 'Is this the man who made the earth tremble, Who shook king-doms, Who made the world as a wilderness And*

destroyed its cities, Who did not open the house of his prisoners?' (Isaiah 14:15-17)

God allows Isaiah to see that one day Satan will be cast into Sheol, the bottomless pit. Notice that people will be amazed to see Satan and they will say, *"Is this the man who made the earth tremble, Who shook kingdoms, Who made the world as a wilderness And destroyed its cities..."* When did Satan do these things? When did the Earth tremble because of Satan? When did the world become a wilderness because of Satan? Could it have happened when God judged Lucifer for his rebellion?

Here is the scenario that seems to have played out. Satan, in his original condition as Lucifer, ruled over God's original creation. When Lucifer rebelled against God, he was judged and cast down to the Earth. This judgment caused the Earth over which Lucifer ruled to be destroyed. The Earth **became** a wilderness, a desolate wasteland, because of the judgment of Lucifer. Whatever cities were here were destroyed. The Earth shook as earthquakes rocked the planet. The light of God which illuminated the Earth was removed and replaced with the darkness of judgment. Water covered the Earth. With His massive judgment for Lucifer's sin of rebellion, God caused the Earth over which Lucifer ruled to change. It turned into the literal depiction found in Genesis 1:2 that we put together earlier from the original Hebrew text, **"And the Earth became a desolate wasteland, empty, without form and covered with darkness."**

Another of God's prophets was allowed to look back in time and see the results of this catastrophic event. God spoke through Jeremiah about the judgment which was coming on the nation of Israel. God is comparing his first judgment against Lucifer to the judgment He will soon bring against Israel.

I beheld the earth, and indeed it was without form, and void; And the heavens, they had no light. (Jeremiah 4:23)

Does this sound familiar? Jeremiah is seeing the Earth as the judgment of Lucifer is taking place.

I beheld the mountains, and indeed they trembled,
And all the hills moved back and forth. (Jeremiah
4:24)

The Earth is rocking with earthquakes which cause an immediate destruction of life on our planet. Could it be that dinosaurs existed in God's original creation and were instantly killed when the Earth quaked and covered the dinosaurs with dirt and sediment? Haven't archaeologists found dinosaur fossils where the creatures still had food in their mouths? How could these creatures die instantly? Was it because of the judgment of Lucifer? Did an ice age begin at that time because of the absence of light and heat? Did this period last millions of years until God put the Earth back in order and provided a new source of light and heat? The Bible isn't absolutely clear on the answers to these questions, but it seems to be a possibility.

I beheld, and indeed there was no man, And all the
birds of the heavens had fled. I beheld, and indeed
the fruitful land was a wilderness, And all its cities
were broken down At the presence of the LORD, By
His fierce anger. (Jeremiah 4:25-26)

The original fruitful creation was destroyed because of God's fierce judgment.

For thus says the LORD: "The whole land shall be
desolate; Yet I will not make a full end. (Jeremiah
4:27)

Now Jeremiah is speaking about the coming judgment of Israel. He says it will be a devastating change but not a complete, full destruction as happened between *Genesis 1:1* and *Genesis 1:2*.

RESTORATION

Now we know what happened to cause the Earth to become **"a desolate wasteland, empty, without form and covered with**

darkness.'' The Bible is not clear on how long the Earth stayed that way. It could have been millions of years. We do know, however, that there came a time when God decided to put the Earth back in order. We find a record of these events in *Genesis 1:3-31*. This new Earth was created for a special being. This being would be different from the angels. He would become the ruler of the new Earth.

CHAPTER 2

TRANSFER OF AUTHORITY

God spent five days creating a magnificent new Earth. He separated the water and the Earth. He made the sun and the moon. He made plants, fish, birds and animals. But on the sixth day, God made something incredible. He made something unlike anything ever created. He made man, His crowning creation, the first human being.

> *Then God said, "Let Us make man in Our image, according to Our likeness; let them have dominion over the fish of the sea, over the birds of the air, and over the cattle, over all the earth and over every creeping thing that creeps on the earth." So God created man in His own image; in the image of God He created him; male and female He created them. Then God blessed them, and God said to them, "Be fruitful and multiply; fill the earth and subdue it; have dominion over the fish of the sea, over the birds of the air, and over every living thing that moves on the earth." (Genesis 1:26-28)*

God created the first man in His own image. What does that mean? How are we like God? Is our body like God? The second chapter of Genesis gives a more detailed version of man's creation.

And the LORD God formed man of the dust of the ground, and breathed into his nostrils the breath of life; and man became a living being. (Genesis 2:7)

Notice that God "formed" man out of the dust of the ground. God formed the human body from the chemical elements He had already created. But God doesn't have a physical body. We know from *John 4:24* that *"God is spirit..."* God is an eternal spirit. God will exist forever. In order to create man in His own image, God had to create an eternal spirit to go in the human body. The physical body God formed had no life in it until God did something very special. After God formed the body, He *"breathed into his nostrils the breath of life; and man became a living being."* When God breathed into the body, He created the human spirit in His own image. Every human being has a spirit. Your spirit is eternal because God is eternal and your spirit is created in His image. Your body houses your spirit, but your body is not the real you. Your spirit is the real you. Your spirit is the part of you which will exist forever. When your body dies, your spirit leaves your body to spend eternity either in the presence of God in Heaven or separated from God in Hell.

After God created man, He said something to his human creation which helps us understand what really happened in the Garden of Eden. He told man He wanted them to rule the Earth. He told Adam and Eve to take dominion over everything on the Earth. This is a critical point. Once God says something, He does not change His mind. That is a good quality. I am glad I do not have to wonder if salvation is still by grace and not by works. I am glad I do not have to ask God every day if trusting in Jesus for my salvation is still good enough. I am glad I can depend on Him to keep His word. When God said mankind was in charge of the Earth, He meant it. He could not back down from what He said.

It was as if God gave man a lease on the Earth He had just created and told them to take good care of it. My wife and I lived in a rental house one time. We signed a one-year lease. The lease agreement gave us the right to live our lives in the house without any interference from the owner. Even though someone else owned the house, the owner could not walk in any time she wanted and fix herself a meal. She could not come in and tell us what to watch on television or how to arrange our furniture. Those decisions were ours to make because we had certain rights that came with having a lease. God still owned the Earth, but He gave a lease to His new creation. They had the right to make decisions about how they conducted their business on the Earth.

> *May you be blessed by the LORD, Who made heaven and earth. The heaven, even the heavens, are the LORD's; But the earth He has given to the children of men. (Psalm 115:15-16)*

God created a beautiful garden for His magnificent creation. He made a place where Adam could be happy and fulfilled. God also gave Adam specific instructions about what to do with the garden.

> *Then the LORD God took the man and put him in the garden of Eden to tend and keep it. (Genesis 2:15)*

God told Adam to tend, or cultivate, the garden. He also told Adam to "keep" the garden. The Hebrew word translated "keep" could also be translated as "guard and protect." The same Hebrew word is used in *Genesis 3:24* to describe the angel who carried a flaming sword *"to guard the way to the tree of life."* God would not tell Adam to do something he was unable to do. He expected Adam to use the dominion God had given him to guard and protect his land from unwelcome intruders. God gave Adam some other instructions, too.

> *And the LORD God commanded the man, saying, "Of every tree of the garden you may freely eat; "but of the tree of the knowledge of good and evil you shall not eat, for in the day that you eat of it you shall surely die." (Genesis 2:16-17)*

These are the only recorded instructions we have from God to Adam to "not do" something. God said "do not" eat of the tree of the knowledge of good and evil. Adam and Eve knew only "good." God is a good God. Adam and Eve were good people. It was their nature to do good because God's nature was in them. They had never experienced anything bad. And God wanted it to stay that way. A complete definition of the Hebrew word translated "evil," as in *"the tree of the knowledge of good and evil,"* is "adversity, affliction, bad, calamity, grief, hurt, harm and trouble." God knew if they ate of the fruit of the tree of the knowledge of good and evil, Adam and Eve would gain the ability to produce evil. God wanted them to produce only good. He did not want them to experience, "adversity, affliction, bad, calamity, grief, hurt, harm and trouble."

THE TEMPTER

Remember Satan? He was cast out of God's presence and lost his position of authority over the Earth. He was no longer beautiful. His access to God was now limited. The Earth he once ruled had become a desolate, dark wasteland because of his rebellion. He may have had millions of years to think about what he had lost. He was there when God put the Earth back in order. He was there when God formed man out of the dust of the Earth. He watched as God breathed into Adam and created his eternal spirit. He also heard God tell Adam to rule the Earth. When Satan heard God say, *"Be fruitful and multiply; fill the earth and subdue it; have dominion over the fish of the sea, over the birds of the air, and over every living thing that moves on the earth,"* something must have stirred deep within him. Ruling the Earth was his old job. He desperately wanted his authority back.

He knew he could not defeat God to get it back. He already tried that and failed miserably. But he also knew something about God. He knew God could only tell the truth and that He could not go back on His word. He had heard God give the Earth to man to rule. The thought must have occurred to him, "If I can get Adam to transfer his authority to me, God can't do anything about it. God has bound Himself by His word. He gave the authority to Adam so Adam is free to do what he pleases with it." Satan developed a plan to regain his lost authority. He decided to borrow the body of an animal and attack Eve first.

SATAN'S TACTICS

The tactics he used on Eve are the same that he uses today. Satan is not very original. When you see how he operated in the Garden of Eden, you will be able to recognize the same strategy he may try to use on you.

> *Now the serpent was more cunning than any beast of the field which the LORD God had made. And he said to the woman, "Has God indeed said, 'You shall not eat of every tree of the garden'?" (Genesis 3:1)*

Satan's first step is to cast doubt on the integrity of God's word. He said to Eve, *"Has God indeed said...?"* He wanted her to question the validity of what God said. He will fire the same thoughts into your head today. He may say things like, "You don't really know what the Bible says. It has been translated so many times, you have no idea what the original text meant." Or he may send someone to you to say, "Those are just man's words. They wrote down some good thoughts, but you can't say those are God's words." Or he may bring up this thought, "The Bible isn't relevant today. Times have changed and those principles don't always apply anymore." If he can get you to disregard God's word, he can feed any kind of thought he wants into your mind and you are likely to believe it.

> *And the woman said to the serpent, "We may eat the fruit of the trees of the garden; "but of the fruit of the tree which is in the midst of the garden, God has said, 'You shall not eat it, nor shall you touch it, lest you die.' " (Genesis 3:2-3)*

Eve makes a terrible mistake by having a conversation with the Devil. We do not need to chat with Satan. Thoughts that come from him should be cast down and totally rejected.

casting down arguments and every high thing that exalts itself against the knowledge of God, bringing every thought into captivity to the obedience of Christ, (2 Corinthians 10:5).

If Satan can get you to talk to him, he will do his best to confuse you. He is a liar. You will not get the truth from Satan. If you want the truth, you will have to talk to God. He is the only one you want to reason with because He will always lead you into the truth.

"Come now, and let us reason together," Says the LORD... (Isaiah 1:18)

Eve made the mistake of reasoning with Satan instead of God. As a result, she got confused about what God said. She misquoted God when she replied to Satan. Eve said that God said, concerning the tree of the knowledge of good and evil, *"You shall not eat it, nor shall you touch it, lest you die."* Is that what God said? No, it is not. God said in *Genesis 2:17, "but of the tree of the knowledge of good and evil you shall not eat, for in the day that you eat of it you shall surely die."* God said they would die if they **ate** the fruit. He did not say they would die if they **touched** the fruit. Satan's plan was working because Eve was reasoning with him and she was confused about what God said. Then Satan became bolder.

Then the serpent said to the woman, "You will not surely die. "For God knows that in the day you eat of it your eyes will be opened, and you will be like God, knowing good and evil." (Genesis 3:4-5)

Satan directly contradicts God and thereby calls God a liar. God said they would die if they ate the fruit. Satan said they would not die if they ate the fruit. Satan is devious, however. He did not start his attack this way. He did not come into the garden and shout to Eve, "You know God is a liar, don't you!" He knew that would not work. So he started by casting doubt on the integrity of the Word of

God. Once Eve got confused about what God said, Satan came in with a direct contradiction.

Immediately after Satan contradicted God, he gave Eve a reason to believe him. He explained that God did not want them to eat the fruit because they would become like God. Isn't that the same problem Lucifer had? He wanted to usurp God's authority and "be like the Most High." He figured he would try the same temptation on Eve. Satan went even farther and said that being like God would include the ability to "know good and evil." Satan, with his twisted, devious logic, explained that they needed to experience both good and evil. Satan feeds them the lie that they can then decide for themselves what is good and evil. Isn't that what God does? The Devil told Eve that God was holding them back. Satan told her to eat of the fruit so she could be wise and make her own decisions about good and evil. Satan uses the same lie today. He tells people, "Do your own thing. It's nobody's business but your own. Have an affair if you want to. Take drugs if it feels good. Live a homosexual lifestyle. Nobody can tell you what to do. Morality is relative. Go ahead and experience those things and then make your own decisions about what is right and wrong." It can be a very intoxicating feeling to be your own god. Many people have bought into that lie. But it is still a lie just like it was with Eve. She is about to find out that there is only one God and He alone decides what is good and evil.

> *So when the woman saw that the tree was good for food, that it was pleasant to the eyes, and a tree desirable to make one wise, she took of its fruit and ate. She also gave to her husband with her, and he ate. Then the eyes of both of them were opened, and they knew that they were naked; and they sewed fig leaves together and made themselves coverings. (Genesis 3:6-7)*

Eve listened to Satan and ate the fruit. Remember the instructions God gave Adam to "guard and protect" the garden? Where was Adam when Satan was talking to his wife? Was he on the other side of the garden eating watermelon? Was he up in a tree playing with the monkeys? The answer is "No" to both of those questions. The Scripture says, after Eve ate the fruit, ***"She also gave to her husband with her, and he ate."*** Adam was right there **"with her."** He heard the whole conversation. God had given Adam dominion over everything on the Earth. God had told Adam to guard and protect the garden. Did Adam use his authority and do what God told him to do? No, he did not. He allowed the Devil to come into his garden and play mind games with his wife. And after his wife ate the forbidden fruit, he did the same thing.

After they ate, ***"Then the eyes of both of them were opened, and they knew that they were naked..."*** Satan's claim was partially true. Their eyes were opened all right. Their physical eyes were already opened so this must mean something else. They became like God in the sense that they perceived their own shame and corruption. They were no longer clothed with the glory of God, but had become mere mortals, subject to death because of their wrong decision.

AUTHORITY LOST

God had given Adam the right to make choices. And Adam made a decision. He decided to listen to Satan instead of God. God said, "Do not eat the fruit." Satan said, "Go ahead and eat the fruit." God has established spiritual laws as well as natural laws to govern our existence. Both were created for our benefit. They always work the way they were created. The law of gravity is an example of a natural law. If you jump off the roof of a house, you will always fall to the ground. No matter how much you want to fly, the force of gravity will pull you toward the center of the Earth and you will hit the ground very quickly. This is a good natural law. Without it, we would all be spinning around in space. Spiritual laws also always work the way they were created. A spiritual law was activated when Adam obeyed Satan and ate the forbidden fruit. This spiritual law is explained in the letter the Holy Spirit inspired Paul to write to the Christians in Rome.

Do you not know that to whom you present your-
selves slaves to obey, you are that one's slaves whom
you obey, whether of sin leading to death, or of
obedience leading to righteousness? (Romans 6:16)

When a person makes a choice to obey someone, he becomes their "slave." A slave has no choice but to obey his master. No matter how the person became a slave, the end result is obedience to the master's wishes. Adam had been given authority over the entire Earth. God gave Adam his authority and, once He gave it, He could not go back on His word and take it back. It was something that belonged to Adam and Adam had a choice about what he did with his authority. Adam's actions created a monumental change in human history. When Adam obeyed Satan, he became a slave to Satan. When Adam ate the forbidden fruit, it is as if he bowed his knee to Satan and handed over the authority of the Earth. Adam chose to become Satan's slave when he chose to obey him instead of God. **Adam gave up his right to rule over Satan when he chose to obey Satan instead of God.** When Adam yielded himself to sin, he became its servant. Adam thereby put his authority in the hands of the author of sin, Satan. Adam became a slave to Satan and the authority of the Earth was transferred into Satan's hands. Deadly consequences followed.

CHAPTER 3

GOD'S PLAN

God told Adam that if he ate the forbidden fruit he would die. A literal interpretation of the Hebrew word translated "die" would read, "in dying you will die." The death God referred to was a spiritual death or a separation from God. Because Adam died spiritually, death also began to work in his physical body and he eventually died physically. That is what God meant when He said, "In dying (spiritually) you will die (physically)." If Adam had never sinned, he would still be alive on the Earth today. God created the human body to live forever. But sin caused the body to become mortal, subject to death. When Adam sinned, he opened the door and allowed sin to enter the pristine new world God had created.

> *Therefore, just as through one man sin entered the world, and death through sin, and thus death spread to all men, because all sinned. (Romans 5:12)*

The *"one man"* who allowed sin to enter the world was Adam. The result of sin entering the world was death, which became a part of every human being's destiny. We all will face physical death one day unless Jesus returns before we die. Spiritual death, separation from God, is also a part of every person's existence because every human being after Adam has sinned.

> *For if by the one man's offense death reigned through the one, much more those who receive abundance of grace and of the gift of righteousness will reign in life through the One, Jesus Christ. (Romans 5:17)*

The *"one man's offense"* was Adam's sin. His offense allowed sin into the world. Sin produces death. Therefore, every person is subject to the reign of death and separation from God because of sin. And Satan is the author of sin. He was the first sinner. He introduced sin to Adam and Eve. Satan rules over every person who has sinned because committing sin makes us a slave of Satan. This ruling or "reigning" of Satan over the Earth continued until Jesus came on the scene. Jesus, we will find out, made it possible for man to once again "reign" over the Devil because of what He accomplished during His time on the Earth. The fact that Satan has authority in the Earth is hard for many people to accept. The Scriptures are clear, however, about Satan's position of authority after Adam's sin.

SATAN'S RULE

After Jesus was baptized by His cousin, John the Baptist, in the Jordan River, Jesus was led by the Holy Spirit into the wilderness for a time of preparation for His public ministry. Jesus fasted for forty days and at the end of His fast we have a record of three temptations Satan brought Him. One of those temptations is critical to demonstrate the truth about Satan's authority.

> *Then the devil, taking Him up on a high mountain, showed Him all the kingdoms of the world in a moment of time. And the devil said to Him, "All this authority I will give You, and their glory; for this has been delivered to me, and I give it to whomever I wish. "Therefore, if You will worship before me, all will be Yours." And Jesus answered and said to him, "Get behind Me, Satan! For it is written, 'You*

34

shall worship the LORD your God, and Him only you shall serve.' " (Luke 4:5-8)

Jesus could tell the difference between the truth and a lie. If this temptation was not true, Jesus would have known and it would not have been a legitimate temptation. Satan's temptation was real. Satan said he had authority over all the kingdoms of the world. Satan said this authority had been delivered to him. Who delivered this authority to Satan? Was it God? Was it Jesus? No, it was Adam. Adam delivered the authority God had given him when he sinned and became a slave of Satan. Jesus responded with God's Word and resisted the Devil's temptation.

But even if our gospel is veiled, it is veiled to those who are perishing, whose minds the god of this age has blinded, who do not believe, lest the light of the gospel of the glory of Christ, who is the image of God, should shine on them. (2 Corinthians 4:3-4)

Paul says unbelievers are not saved because their minds have been blinded. If you are blind, you cannot see. Unsaved people have not been able to see the light of Jesus. They have not comprehended His incredible grace and mercy. Who would want to keep people from knowing about Jesus? Who would want to keep people from being saved? Satan! Satan, God's enemy since He cast him out of Heaven, wants to keep people from experiencing God's forgiveness. Satan is referred to as *"the god of this age."* A "god" is a ruler, isn't he? The Greek word translated "age" is "aion." It means "an age, a period of time." Adam was the original "god" or "ruler" of the Earth. Now, Satan is the ruler of the Earth, but only for a certain period of time. There is an appointed time for his reign to end, but for now he has to be dealt with. He is "god" or "ruler" over those who have not been saved and he wants to keep them blinded so he can take them to Hell with him. How did he become the "god of this age?" Adam's sin gave Satan authority to reign over those controlled by sin.

> *We know that we are of God, and the whole world lies*
> *under the sway of the wicked one. (1 John 5:19)*

> *We know that we are of God, and that the whole world*
> *lies in the power of the evil one. (1 John 5:19)(NAS)*

> *We know [positively] that we are of God, and the*
> *whole world [around us] is under the power of the*
> *evil one. (1 John 5:19)(AMP)*

How did the world get in the power of Satan, the evil, wicked one? Adam handed the world over to him! People ask, "Why is there so much evil in the world?" Look who is in control. Satan is still in control of many people. He is a liar and a murderer. Satan influences people to do evil. Satan hates God and wants to destroy His creation. God is sovereign, but He has bound Himself by His word. God gave authority to run the Earth to Adam and Adam gave it to Satan. I know this is bad news. But you have to understand the bad news first to fully comprehend the good news of what Jesus did for us! You will soon find out that Satan no longer rules over those who have been born again.

GOD'S PLAN

> *For this reason I bow my knees to the Father of our*
> *Lord Jesus Christ, from whom the whole family in*
> *heaven and earth is named, (Ephesians 3:14-15)*

God's original intention was to have a family. He planned to love and care for His family. He enjoyed coming down to the Earth in the late afternoon to visit with His new creation, Adam and Eve (*Genesis 3:8*). His will did not change because of the tragedy which happened in the Garden of Eden. He just made a new way to become part of the family. He refers to Christians as His family members. We have members living all over the Earth as well as in Heaven. But we are all part of the same family. One day we will have a gigantic family reunion. Many families hold family reunions every year. Sometimes it is hard to keep track of who is who. "Let's see, are you my third cousin once removed or my second cousin by marriage or ..." There is one good thing about our reunion in Heaven. We will all be brothers and sisters. No cousins or aunts or uncles. We have all been born from above with the same Father and we are all in the same family.

Even though Adam and Eve disrupted His original plan, God was ready with a new plan. Satan thought he had won when he persuaded Adam to sin. But God was way ahead of Satan's schemes. After God exposed Adam and Eve's sin, He began to talk about His new plan.

> *So the LORD God said to the serpent: "Because you have done this, You are cursed more than all cattle, And more than every beast of the field; On your belly you shall go, And you shall eat dust All the days of your life. And I will put enmity Between you and the woman, And between your seed and her Seed; He shall bruise your head, And you shall bruise His heel." (Genesis 3:14-15)*

God started talking to the serpent, whose body the Devil had used, but He quickly began to address His comments directly to Satan. God said there would be enmity, or conflict, between Satan's seed, or offspring, and the Seed of the woman. God then says this mysterious "Seed of the woman" will "bruise" Satan's "head." This creates a word picture of a person stomping on the head of a snake with his heel. The action causes the snake's head to be bruised as well as the heel of the person doing the stomping. This is a good picture of Jesus' ultimate defeat of Satan, but there is more to this statement than a word picture. The word "head," as in *"He shall bruise your head"* is an oriental term which refers to authority. We still use it today when we refer to the president of a company as the "head" of the company. The "head" person in any group is the person with the most authority. God said there would come a day when the "Seed of the woman" will "bruise" the head of the Devil. The Hebrew word translated "bruise" can also be translated "break." God is saying there will come a day when the Seed of the woman will break the authority Satan took from Adam. The Seed of the woman is going to regain what Adam just lost.

Satan did not understand who the Seed of the woman would be. One thing Satan did know, however, was that God always kept His word. Satan knew that because God said it, whoever this "Seed of the woman" is will certainly break the hold he had on man because of sin. From that day forward, Satan began to look for the Seed.

Imagine a mafia boss telling you that a hit man has been assigned to kill you. Would you live your life any differently? I would! I would look out the window before I left the house to make sure nobody was lurking outside to shoot me. I would look underneath my car to be certain a bomb had not been attached. I would look in the back seat of the car to find out if the hit man was in there. When I walked down the street, I would constantly be on the lookout to see who was walking toward me or who was coming out of an alley. I would live my life looking over my shoulder to avoid the hit man who had been promised.

SATAN'S TORMENT

This is what happened to Satan after he heard these words from God. He knew the "Seed" would defeat him so he decided he had to eliminate the "Seed" before the "Seed" had a chance to take back his authority. He began to be on the lookout to find the "Seed." When Eve gave birth to her first child, Satan was listening to what she said.

> *Now Adam knew Eve his wife, and she conceived and bore Cain, and said, "I have acquired a man from the LORD." Then she bore again, this time his brother Abel. Now Abel was a keeper of sheep, but Cain was a tiller of the ground. (Genesis 4:1-2)*

Eve said this child was, **"a man from the Lord."** Satan surely wondered, "Could this be the coming Seed? Will he be the one to defeat me?" After these two children grew up, Satan planted a thought in Cain's mind to kill his brother Abel. Once Cain sinned by killing his brother, he was under the control of Satan and was no longer a threat. If Cain was the "Seed," Satan thought he had thwarted God's plan.

Much later on, Satan hears God make promises to bless Abraham and his descendants. Abraham has a son named Isaac who has a son named Jacob. Jacob has an encounter with God and God changes Jacob's name to Israel. Israel has twelve sons, one whose name is Joseph. Joseph's brothers are jealous of him and sell him as a slave. God has His hand on Joseph and causes him to be elevated to second-in-command under Pharaoh in Egypt. When a famine comes to the land, Joseph has Egypt prepared. God had revealed to him to store grain for seven years because of the coming famine. Joseph brings his family to live in Egypt so he can take care of them. After Pharaoh dies and Joseph dies, the Israelites, the descendants of Joseph's father, Israel, multiply so much that the new Pharaoh becomes fearful that Israel will turn against him. Satan knows the Seed will come out of Israel's descendants. So he plants a thought in Pharaoh's head which will eliminate the possibility of the Seed interfering with Satan's dominance. Pharaoh issues a horrible command concerning the people of Israel.

> ***So Pharaoh commanded all his people, saying, "Every son who is born you shall cast into the river, and every daughter you shall save alive." (Exodus 1:22)***

Because of this decree, a loving Israelite mother placed her baby boy in a basket in the river near Pharaoh's house. Moses, the baby boy, was rescued by Pharaoh's daughter and raised in Pharaoh's home. Satan was not able to stop Moses from growing into a great deliverer. Moses eventually led the nation of Israel out of the bondage of Egypt.

Satan tried to have the entire nation of Israel destroyed another time. King Ahasuerus had gotten mad at his wife because she wouldn't parade before his drunken friends at a drinking party. The King decided to get rid of his wife and find a new queen. After a search of his kingdom for the most beautiful women, the finalists were pampered for a year to prepare for their presentation to the king. A beautiful Jewish woman named Esther was one of the women chosen. When the king first saw Esther, he immediately fell in love with her and made her his new queen. Esther had been raised by her older cousin, Mordecai, after her parents died. Esther had not told the king she was a Jew.

Through a complicated series of events, the king was persuaded to sign a hideous decree. The king decreed that every Jewish person was to be destroyed on a certain date. Who do you think was behind this scheme? Satan is still looking for the Seed. He has to destroy the Seed before the Seed destroys him. Mordecai told Esther she must approach the king and tell him the error of his ways. She had to tell him she was a Jew who would be killed according to his decree. Esther successfully persuaded the king to rescind his decree and the nation of Israel was once again protected by God. (See the book of Esther)

Prophecies came forth from the prophet Isaiah that an anointed ruler will be a descendant of both Jesse and Jesse's son, David (*Isaiah 11:1-2 and 9:6-7*). During King Saul's reign, the prophet Samuel publicly anointed David, a teenager at the time, to be the next king (*1 Samuel 16:12-13*). Satan decides that if he can destroy David, then this anointed ruler will never be born. David grows up to be an intensely loyal staff member to King Saul. But Satan is out to destroy the Seed. Satan inspires King Saul to have a jealous hatred for David and to spend many years trying to kill him (*1 Samuel 18-31*). David wrote many of the Psalms while he was on the run from Saul. But God protected David and he eventually assumed the throne after Saul was killed in battle.

THE SEED – KING JESUS

Finally, it is time for the Seed to actually appear on the scene. When Jesus was born in Bethlehem, a sign appeared in the sky. Some men came to Jerusalem and asked King Herod where they could find the King of the Jews. King Herod asked his staff where the Messiah had been prophesied to be born. They told him the Messiah was to be born in Bethlehem. King Herod was afraid this new king would be a threat to him so he made up a story to tell the men seeking to find Jesus.

And he sent them to Bethlehem and said, "Go and search carefully for the young Child, and when you have found Him, bring back word to me, that I may come and worship Him also." (Matthew 2:8)

King Herod had no intention of worshipping Jesus. He wanted to eliminate his rival as soon as possible. The men followed the star that led them to Jesus. After they presented their gifts, they did not go back to tell King Herod how to find Jesus. They went another direction.

When they heard the king, they departed; and behold, the star which they had seen in the East went before them, till it came and stood over where the young Child was. When they saw the star, they rejoiced with exceedingly great joy. And when they had come into the house, they saw the young Child with Mary His mother, and fell down and worshiped Him. And when they had opened their treasures, they presented gifts to Him: gold, frankincense, and myrrh. Then, being divinely warned in a dream that they should not return to Herod, they departed for their own country another way. (Matthew 2:9-12)

King Herod finally figured out the men were not coming back to tell him where to find Jesus. Satan brought back one of his old schemes and planted a thought in Herod's mind. He told him to kill all the male children under two years old. Since it had been less than two years since the King of the Jews was born, he figured that would certainly eliminate the Seed of the woman.

Then Herod, when he saw that he was deceived by the wise men, was exceedingly angry; and he sent forth and put to death all the male children who were in Bethlehem and in all its districts, from two years old and under, according to the time which he had determined from the wise men. (Matthew 2:16)

As usual, God was way ahead of Satan. After the wise men left, God sent an angel to warn Joseph and give instructions on how to escape the wrath of King Herod.

> *Now when they had departed, behold, an angel of the Lord appeared to Joseph in a dream, saying, "Arise, take the young Child and His mother, flee to Egypt, and stay there until I bring you word; for Herod will seek the young Child to destroy Him." (Matthew 2:13)*

Jesus grew up in relative obscurity. Satan apparently did not know what happened to this child who was born with such fanfare. But when Jesus was approximately thirty years old, He came face to face with Satan. Jesus was ready to begin His public ministry. He had been baptized in water by John the Baptist. God gave John a divine revelation that Jesus was the promised Messiah. When John the Baptist saw Jesus approaching him to be baptized in the Jordan River, John shouted, *...Behold! The Lamb of God who takes away the sin of the world! (John 1:29)*. After Jesus was baptized, the Holy Spirit led Him into the wilderness to spend an extended period of time in prayer and preparation. Jesus fasted for 40 days. Satan realized his opportunities to eliminate the Seed were diminishing rapidly. He tried a desperate measure.

> *Then the devil took Him up into the holy city, set Him on the pinnacle of the temple, and said to Him, "If You are the Son of God, throw Yourself down. For it is written: 'He shall give His angels charge over you,' and, 'In their hands they shall bear you up, Lest you dash your foot against a stone.'" Jesus said to him, "It is written again, 'You shall not tempt the LORD your God.'" (Matthew 4:5-7)*

Satan tried to get Jesus to commit suicide! He tells him to jump off the top of the temple. He distorts Scripture to try to make Jesus think the angels will catch Him if He jumps. Jesus sees through his tactics, though, and refuses to tempt God to save Him from such a foolish act.

Then Satan tempts Jesus with the very thing Jesus came to regain. Satan tempts Jesus by offering the authority Satan had been given by Adam.

> *Again, the devil took Him up on an exceedingly high mountain, and showed Him all the kingdoms of the world and their glory. And he said to Him, "All these things I will give You if You will fall down and worship me." Then Jesus said to him, "Away with you, Satan! For it is written, 'You shall worship the LORD your God, and Him only you shall serve.' " (Matthew 4:8-10)*

Satan is a master of mixing truth with lies. Satan offered Jesus authority in the Earth. It was true that Satan had the authority. But it was not true that Jesus could get it back by worshipping Satan. Satan knew if Jesus obeyed him, He would become a sinner, and God's plan would be foiled. Jesus once again rejected Satan's temptation. Jesus actually already had the authority Satan was offering. But it was not because Jesus was God. It was something else which we will reveal in the coming chapters.

CHAPTER 4

THE COVENANT

God spoke to Satan about the "Seed of the woman" in *Genesis 3:15*. God said this Seed would "bruise" or "break" Satan's headship or authority. Just who is this Seed and why would He be able to regain the authority man had lost? In order to understand how this works, we have to remember God's words to Adam. God gave the Earth to Adam and told him to run things with the authority God had given him. Since God had put His word on the line, He could only work within the bounds of His word to gain an entrance back into the Earth. He would not destroy Adam and Eve because He gave them the right to make choices. Even though they made the wrong choice, God's word still could not be violated.

Since God gave the authority of the Earth to a man, He would have to work through a man to gain it back. In order for God to have an entrance back into the affairs of mankind without violating His word, He would need a voluntary agreement with man. A covenant is the strongest agreement ever invented. A covenant agreement is an all-out commitment between two entities. A covenant could be between two people, two tribes or two countries. When two people establish a covenant, each party is saying, "Whatever I have, if you need it, it is yours. And whatever you have, if I need it, it is mine."

This worked well for countries or tribes which had different strengths or weaknesses. For example, Tribe A may be made up of fierce warriors. They can win most any battle they undertake. But they have a weakness in growing crops to provide food. Tribe B may be well-schooled in growing crops, but they do not have a propensity for fighting. As a result, Tribe A is hungry most of the time and Tribe B has their food stolen by other tribes that can fight better. These two tribes decide to "cut a covenant." It is referred to in this manner because blood must be shed to establish the covenant relationship.

Once the covenant is established, this is how it would work. When Tribe A comes home from winning a great battle, they are hungry. They look to Tribe B to provide food because a covenant means, "whatever I need, if you have it, it is mine." The food produced by Tribe B is no longer their own. It now belongs to Tribe A when they need it.

When Tribe B is attacked by another tribe, they look to Tribe A to help them because of their covenant. Tribe A is obligated to provide their fighting expertise to defend Tribe B in their time of need. This makes for a good arrangement. One tribe provides most of the food and the other tribe provides protection for the food.

God chose a man by the name of Abram with which to establish His covenant and gain an entrance back into the Earth. The record of God speaking to this man begins in Genesis.

> *Now the LORD had said to Abram: "Get out of your country, From your family And from your father's house, To a land that I will show you. I will make you a great nation; I will bless you And make your name great; And you shall be a blessing. I will bless those who bless you, And I will curse him who curses you; And in you all the families of the earth shall be blessed." So Abram departed as the LORD had spoken to him, and Lot went with him. And Abram was seventy-five years old when he departed from Haran. (Genesis 12:1-4)*

God began by telling Abram he must leave home. He did not tell him where his journey would end. But God told Abram how He would bless him and protect him. In the incident shown above, God was beginning to reveal His part of the covenant relationship even though He had not yet told Abram about the covenant. The next time we have a record of God speaking to Abram is after Abram has rescued his nephew Lot and Lot's family from being taken captive.

> *After these things the word of the LORD came to Abram in a vision, saying, "Do not be afraid, Abram. I am your shield, your exceedingly great reward." But Abram said, "Lord GOD, what will You give me, seeing I go childless, and the heir of my house is Eliezer of Damascus?" Then Abram said, "Look, You have given me no offspring; indeed one born in my house is my heir!" And behold, the word of the LORD came to him, saying, "This one shall not be your heir, but one who will come from your own body shall be your heir." Then He brought him outside and said, "Look now toward heaven, and count the stars if you are able to number them." And He said to him, "So shall your descendants be." And he believed in the LORD, and He accounted it to him for righteousness. (Genesis 15:1-6)*

Abram was beginning to wonder how God could bless all his descendants when Abram had no children. That is why he asked if his servant would have to be his heir. But God reinforced His promise by using a visual demonstration. He told Abram his descendants would be more than he could possibly number. In *Genesis 15:9-10*, God told Abram to shed the blood of animals to establish His covenant.

> *On the same day the LORD made a covenant with Abram, saying: "To your descendants I have given this land, from the river of Egypt to the great river, the River Euphrates— (Genesis 15:18)*

Twenty-four years after God first spoke to Abram about blessing his descendants, Abram was still childless. His wife, Sarai, never was able to have children all through her normal child-bearing years.

Now, she is old, and Abram is 99 years old. God still has plans for Abram and his descendants and He reminds him of the covenant.

> *When Abram was ninety-nine years old, the LORD appeared to Abram and said to him, "I am Almighty God; walk before Me and be blameless. "And I will make My covenant between Me and you, and will multiply you exceedingly." Then Abram fell on his face, and God talked with him, saying: "As for Me, behold, My covenant is with you, and you shall be a father of many nations. "No longer shall your name be called Abram, but your name shall be Abraham; for I have made you a father of many nations. "I will make you exceedingly fruitful; and I will make nations of you, and kings shall come from you. "And I will establish My covenant between Me and you and your descendants after you in their generations, for an everlasting covenant, to be God to you and your descendants after you. (Genesis 17:1-7)*

God changes Abram's name to Abraham, which means, "father of a multitude." To the natural mind, this seems foolish. Every time someone called Abraham by his new name, they were saying, "father of a multitude." This was to a man who was 99 years old and whose wife was barren. But once God says something, it will come to pass if we believe it. We can depend on His word. And it happened just as God said.

> *And the LORD visited Sarah as He had said, and the LORD did for Sarah as He had spoken. For Sarah conceived and bore Abraham a son in his old age, at the set time of which God had spoken to him. And Abraham called the name of his son who was born to him—whom Sarah bore to him—Isaac. Then Abraham circumcised his son Isaac when he was eight days old, as God had commanded him. Now Abraham was one hundred years old when his son*

Isaac was born to him. And Sarah said, "God has made me laugh, and all who hear will laugh with me." She also said, "Who would have said to Abraham that Sarah would nurse children? For I have borne him a son in his old age." (Genesis 21:1-7)

PROVING THE COVENANT

The promise of the covenant is fulfilled. God did what He said He would do. But there are two sides to a covenant. Each person must do his part or the covenant is of no value. God is gaining entrance back into the Earth without violating His word. He is working with a man -- a man with whom He has made a covenant. A number of years after Isaac was born, God placed what seemed like an unrealistic demand on Abraham.

Now it came to pass after these things that God tested Abraham, and said to him, "Abraham!" And he said, "Here I am." Then He said, "Take now your son, your only son Isaac, whom you love, and go to the land of Moriah, and offer him there as a burnt offering on one of the mountains of which I shall tell you." (Genesis 22:1-2)

This is an incredible event. Abraham waited 25 years for the beginning of the fulfillment of the promise God made to him. God said He would bless Abraham's descendants. God said he would have more descendants than he could count. They would be more than the sand on the beach, more than the stars in the sky. All of this would start with Isaac. Abraham surely was enjoying his time with Isaac. They played and laughed together. They worked and sweated together. Abraham was teaching him all the things a father loves to teach his son. Isaac adored his father and Abraham was thrilled with the wonderful gift God had given him at 100 years of age. Abraham looked forward to watching his son grow into manhood. And then God told Abraham to kill his son. There is no other way to put it. A burnt offering is killed and then burnt.

God, what are you doing to Abraham? What kind of a reward is this for trusting you for 25 years? How could you do such a thing? Those thoughts went through my mind as I read this passage of Scripture for the first time. But that was before I understood the terms of a covenant. Notice very carefully what God said. *"Now it came to pass after these things that God tested Abraham..."* "Test" means "to determine the quality of by testing." In order for a covenant to be valid, both parties had to be able to fulfill their responsibilities. God had to "prove" that Abraham would uphold his part of the covenant by giving God whatever He needed. If Abraham was unwilling to keep the covenant, the agreement had no value and God would have no access back into the affairs of man.

Let me illustrate what I am saying. If the Department of Transportation (DOT) for your state decided a 5-mile stretch of highway and bridges needed to be rebuilt, they would advertise for bids. Let's say the DOT engineers have estimated the cost of the work to be $10 million. When the due date arrives, the DOT representative opens the bids. One says $11.1 million. Another says $9.9 million. One says $10.4 million. Then my bid is opened. My bid says I can do the job for $150,000. Since I am the low bidder, does that mean I have to be awarded the bid? Not necessarily. First, I have to prove I am capable of doing the job. The DOT representative will ask me some questions.

"Mr. Clark, do you have experience in this kind of work?"

"No, I don't," I would say.

Mr. Clark, do you have the heavy equipment necessary to remove the top layer of existing asphalt?"

"No sir, I don't own any equipment."

"Mr. Clark, do you have the capability to produce asphalt or do you have a contract with an existing asphalt plant?"

"No, I do not."

Mr. Clark, do you have the equipment necessary to put down the new asphalt?"

"No, I do not."

"Mr. Clark, do you have a crew of employees experienced in this kind of work?"

"No, I don't have any employees at all."

"Mr. Clark, how do you expect to perform the work described in this bid document?"

"I thought I would just hire some folks and figure it out as I went along."

Do you think the DOT would award the contract to me? Of course not. The DOT "tested" or "proved" me and found I was not capable of performing the contract. Even if both parties signed the contract, it would be of no value.

The same thing happens when you purchase a house. The mortgage company will make you prove you are capable of performing your part of the mortgage contract. They make you prove you earn enough money to pay the monthly mortgage amount. They will probably make you show them a paycheck stub just to prove you are telling the truth about how much money you make. If your monthly salary is the same as the house payment, you cannot fulfill your part of the contract and still feed and clothe your family. The mortgage company would not grant a mortgage under those circumstances.

Just because God established a covenant with Abraham did not make it valid. Abraham had to prove he was capable of performing the terms of the covenant. Remember, a covenant means, "Whatever I have, if you need it, I am **obligated** to give it to you." God made a demand on Abraham according to the covenant. It was up to Abraham to prove he would do what was required.

So Abraham rose early in the morning and saddled his donkey, and took two of his young men with him, and Isaac his son; and he split the wood for the burnt offering, and arose and went to the place of which God had told him. (Genesis 22:3)

This is a wonderful picture of Abraham's 100 percent commitment to God. As Isaac is growing up and Abraham is enjoying life, God speaks to him to kill his precious son. Most people would have wanted some time to think about it. If I had been in Abraham's shoes, I probably would have asked God if I could do that "next year." But what was Abraham's reaction? The next morning Abraham is already obeying God. He cuts the wood for the fire and takes two assistants with him as they head to the mountain.

> *Then on the third day Abraham lifted his eyes and saw the place afar off. And Abraham said to his young men, "Stay here with the donkey; the lad and I will go yonder and worship, and we will come back to you." (Genesis 22:4-5)*

Abraham makes an interesting statement here. He says to his two assistants, *"the lad and I will go yonder and worship, and we will come back to you."* Why did he say, *"we"* will come back? Didn't God tell him to sacrifice his son? Doesn't sacrifice mean "kill and burn on the altar?" Did Abraham really intend to kill his son as God had commanded? I believe Abraham certainly did intend to kill his son. The explanation of his statement to his assistants will be revealed shortly.

> *So Abraham took the wood of the burnt offering and laid it on Isaac his son; and he took the fire in his hand, and a knife, and the two of them went together. But Isaac spoke to Abraham his father and said, "My father!" And he said, "Here I am, my son." Then he said, "Look, the fire and the wood, but where is the lamb for a burnt offering?" And Abraham said, "My son, God will provide for Himself the lamb for a burnt offering." So the two of them went together. (Genesis 22:6-8)*

How Abraham's heart must have ached as he heard his son ask him about the sacrifice! We read these words in a few seconds without understanding the incredible emotional turmoil which must have been raging in Abraham's soul. His son, whom he had waited on for 25 years, would soon be dead by his father's own hand.

> *Then they came to the place of which God had told him. And Abraham built an altar there and placed*

the wood in order; and he bound Isaac his son and laid him on the altar, upon the wood. (Genesis 22:9)

We do not know for sure Isaac's age at this point. Some say he was in his teens and some say he could have been older. Abraham was well over 100 years old when he tied Isaac up and put him on the altar. Don't you think Isaac could have run off down the hill and his elderly father could never have caught him? But he didn't do that. Isaac reverenced his father and obediently allowed himself to be bound and placed on the altar. By now Isaac knew **he** was the sacrifice.

And Abraham stretched out his hand and took the knife to slay his son. (Genesis 22:10)

Abraham faced the moment of truth. Would he go through with this act? Would he plunge the knife into his only son's body and kill him as God had commanded? To understand what happened next, you have to understand that God sees people differently than we do. God can see into your heart. God can see your motivation and your intentions. He later told Samuel, the prophet, in *1 Samuel 16:7, "... For the LORD does not see as man sees; for man looks at the outward appearance, but the LORD looks at the heart."* We sometimes try to hide our true intentions. Jesus addressed that subject in *Matthew 5:27-28,* when He said, *"You have heard that it was said to those of old, 'You shall not commit adultery.' "But I say to you that whoever looks at a woman to lust for her has already committed adultery with her in his heart."* I believe Jesus was saying that adultery is committed when the decision is made in the heart. When a man looks at a woman and decides to commit adultery with her, he has already sinned because God saw the decision in the heart. It is then only a matter of time until the man works out the details to complete the physical act he has already decided to commit.

Abraham is standing over his son with his knife drawn. God is looking into Abraham's heart to see if he has made the decision to fully obey God and kill his son. Will Abraham be proven willing and able to maintain a covenant with God? What about the statement Abraham made to his assistants that he and the lad would return?

How could he truly be planning to kill and burn his son, yet say they would both return? The answer is found in the New Testament book of Hebrews. The writer of Hebrews is listing men who have performed great feats of faith. He begins by talking about Abraham and he gives us a revelation about Abraham's thought process during this crisis in his life.

> *By faith Abraham, when he was tested, offered up Isaac, and he who had received the promises offered up his only begotten son, of whom it was said, "In Isaac your seed shall be called," concluding that God was able to raise him up, even from the dead, from which he also received him in a figurative sense. (Hebrews 11:17-19)*

Remember that Abraham had relied on God's promise of nations of descendants for 25 years. God told him it would all start with Isaac. But God also told him to kill Isaac as a sacrifice. Abraham knew God's word had to happen. He knew it was not possible for God to lie. He believed that God's promise **had** to come to pass. Abraham thought he knew how it would happen. He knew he had to obey God and kill his son. **He figured the only way God's word could be fulfilled would be for Isaac to be raised from the dead.** He pictured this scenario in his mind, in a "figurative sense." That is why he told his assistants they would "both" come back. It was not because he would refuse to kill his son. It was because he had pictured God raising his son from the dead after he killed him.

God had another plan in mind, however. Abraham did not understand about God looking into the heart. Abraham was prepared mentally and physically to use his knife to take his son's life. God saw that the decision was made and Abraham was a split second away from plunging the knife into his son's body.

> *But the Angel of the LORD called to him from heaven and said, "Abraham, Abraham!" So he said, "Here I am." And He said, "Do not lay your hand on the lad, or do anything to him; for now I know*

that you fear God, since you have not withheld your son, your only son, from Me." Then Abraham lifted his eyes and looked, and there behind him was a ram caught in a thicket by its horns. So Abraham went and took the ram, and offered it up for a burnt offering instead of his son. And Abraham called the name of the place, The- LORD -WILL-PROVIDE; as it is said to this day, "In the Mount of The LORD it shall be provided." (Genesis 22:11-14)

God stopped Abraham from killing his son. His heart had been tested and he had proven to the entire universe that he would keep the covenant. God told the angel to say to Abraham on God's behalf, *"you have not withheld your son, your only son, from Me."* This is a pivotal point in history. **A covenant relationship requires that both parties be willing to provide what the other needs.** Abraham was the representative of the human race with whom God had chosen to establish a covenant. God had required that Abraham offer "his son, his only son" to prove the covenant.

THIS OPENED THE DOOR FOR GOD, THE OTHER PARTNER IN THE COVENANT, TO OFFER TO MANKIND "HIS ONLY BEGOTTEN SON" WHEN WE HAD NEED OF HIM TO REMOVE OUR SINS.

Then the Angel of the LORD called to Abraham a second time out of heaven, and said: "By Myself I have sworn, says the LORD, because you have done this thing, and have not withheld your son, your only son— "blessing I will bless you, and multiplying I will multiply your descendants as the stars of the heaven and as the sand which is on the seashore; and your descendants shall possess the gate of their enemies. "In your seed all the nations of the earth shall be blessed, because you have obeyed My voice." (Genesis 22:15-18)

The angel continues to deliver God's word and divine revelation to Abraham. He reiterates God's covenant promise. He says Abraham's descendants *"shall possess the gate of their enemies."* The descendants he refers to are not just Abraham's physical lineage, as we will see later. What does it mean to possess the gate of your enemies? In ancient times, such as when Abraham lived, many cities were surrounded by walls. These walls were for protection from their enemies. If an army was approaching to attack the city, the gate-keepers would close the gates. This would eliminate the possibility of the enemy easily overrunning the city by rushing through the open gates. The gatekeeper held a very important position. He could effectively control the domain inside the walls by making sure the gate was shut when the city was threatened. The opposition forces who wanted to control the domain inside the walls knew they had to attack the gate first. If they could gain control of the gate, they could control the city. God said through his angel that Abraham's descendants would possess the gates of their enemies. That meant they will control the domain of their enemies instead of their enemies controlling them. All this will be made possible by the "Seed."

The "Seed" referred to here has a natural application and a spiritual application. The natural part describes Abraham's natural descendants. The spiritual side describes the Seed we have been talking about since God told Satan the Seed would bruise his head.

> *Now to Abraham and his Seed were the promises made. He does not say, "And to seeds," as of many, but as of one, "And to your Seed," who is Christ. (Galatians 3:16)*

THE SEED REFERS TO JESUS CHRIST! He is the one who will break Satan's authority over the human race. Jesus came to fulfill the promise God made in Genesis 3:15.

> *[But] he who commits sin [who practices evildoing] is of the devil [takes his character from the evil one], for the devil has sinned (violated the divine law) from the beginning. The reason the Son of God*

was made manifest (visible) was to undo (destroy, loosen, and dissolve) the works the devil [has done]. (1 John 3:8)(AMP)

Jesus came to **totally destroy** Satan's authority to put man in bondage to sin, sickness, fear, poverty and every evil work. But how did He do it? How did the Seed come into the Earth?

CHAPTER 5

JESUS, THE MAN

God promised Satan that He would take back the authority Adam handed over to Satan in the Garden of Eden. But God gave the authority to rule the Earth to Adam, to mankind. So how could God get it back without violating His word?

God gave the prophet Isaiah a glimpse into the future to perceive a miraculous event which would take place. I am sure those who heard him speak these words had no idea what he was talking about. They may have thought he had lost his mind. What he was describing seemed to make no sense at all.

> *"Therefore the Lord Himself will give you a sign: Behold, the virgin shall conceive and bear a Son, and shall call His name Immanuel. (Isaiah 7:14)*

How can a virgin conceive and bear a child? God was revealing how the Seed of the woman would be manifested. He said they would call His name, "Immanuel," which means, "God with us." God gave the authority over the Earth to a man. Therefore, He would have to gain the authority back through a man. But there seemed to be a huge problem with that concept. Every man was a sinner.

> *Therefore, just as through one man sin entered the world, and death through sin, and thus death spread to all men, because all sinned— (Romans 5:12)*

When Adam disobeyed God, sin entered the world. Sin produces death, which is separation from God. Sin and its result, death, spread to all men who would ever be born. Every human being is born infected with sin. This sin infection will always manifest itself. A newborn baby is not born a sinner. A baby cannot sin. But the child is infected with sin. That means there will come a day when the child will sin. The child will willingly disobey his parents or teacher and will sin. He can't help it. He is infected with sin because of Adam's disobedience.

God had to take back the authority from Satan through a man. But every man is a sinner and, therefore, a slave to the author of sin, Satan. That is why God could not simply pick a man and help him live a sinless life. No human being born after Adam could keep from sinning. But God had a plan to manifest the Seed of the woman. To understand how God did it, we have to understand the truth about faith and the word of God.

> *Now faith is the substance of things hoped for, the evidence of things not seen. For by it the elders obtained a good testimony. By faith we understand that the worlds were framed by the word of God, so that the things which are seen were not made of things which are visible. (Hebrews 11:1-3)*

The worlds were "framed" by the word of God. The Bible says in *Genesis 1:2* that *"the Spirit of God was hovering over the face of the waters."* Then the Bible describes how God "spoke" the worlds into existence. The Holy Spirit, the power of God, was not actively doing anything but "hovering." But once God spoke, the Holy Spirit went into action and caused God's words to be manifested. The word of God spoken in faith activated the Holy Spirit. The Holy Spirit took God's faith-filled words and powerfully caused them to become a physical reality.

"For My thoughts are not your thoughts, Nor are your ways My ways," says the LORD. "For as the heavens are higher than the earth, So are My ways higher than your ways, And My thoughts than your thoughts. "For as the rain comes down, and the snow from heaven, And do not return there, But water the earth, And make it bring forth and bud, That it may give seed to the sower And bread to the eater, So shall My word be that goes forth from My mouth; It shall not return to Me void, But it shall accomplish what I please, And it shall prosper in the thing for which I sent it. (Isaiah 55:8-11)

God said His word would not return to Him void (or without result). He said it would accomplish what He intended for it to accomplish. His word has the capability to cause itself to come to pass when someone will believe it.

For the word of God is living and powerful, and sharper than any two-edged sword, piercing even to the division of soul and spirit, and of joints and marrow, and is a discerner of the thoughts and intents of the heart. (Hebrews 4:12)

The Bible is much more than a history book. It is a record of the living, powerful word of God. There is a difference between the leather-bound book someone may carry to church services and the word of God. The Bible we carry is only leather and paper and ink. Your Bible probably says "Holy Bible" on it somewhere. The word of God truly is holy, but your Bible, a record of the word of God, is not. Some folks won't write in their Bible because they think it would be sacrilegious. If you cannot write in your Bible, seal it up under glass so no one can touch it and go buy a Bible you can use. Your Bible should be your handbook for life. The pages should be wrinkled and yellow from use. Are your Bible pages still stuck together like the day you bought it? Your Bible should have notes in the margins of things you have learned about God from that page.

The true word of God, however, is a living thing. It is full of the life of God. It is full of the power of God.

Jesus told a parable in the 4th Chapter of the gospel of Mark. The parable describes a man who went out to sow (or plant) seeds in the ground. When Jesus explained the meaning of the parable, He gave us additional insight into the life and power in the word of God. He explained that the seed the man planted represented the word of God.

The sower sows the word. (Mark 4:14)

Jesus compares the word of God to a seed. A seed is a small substance which contains life. A tomato seed contains the life of a tomato. When a tomato seed is planted in the proper environment, it will produce tomatoes. The seed has the life within it to produce what it was created to produce. The word of God is like a seed. It contains the life of God and is programmed to produce what it was created to produce. If it is planted in the proper environment, a faith-filled heart, it will produce.

Now that we have established the power of the word of God, we can understand how God was able to enter the Earth as a man without sin. The Christmas story will have a whole new meaning for you after you finish this chapter.

> *Now in the sixth month the angel Gabriel was sent by God to a city of Galilee named Nazareth, to a virgin betrothed to a man whose name was Joseph, of the house of David. The virgin's name was Mary. And having come in, the angel said to her, "Rejoice, highly favored one, the Lord is with you; blessed are you among women!" But when she saw him, she was troubled at his saying, and considered what manner of greeting this was. Then the angel said to her, "Do not be afraid, Mary, for you have found favor with God. "And behold, you will conceive in your womb and bring forth a Son, and shall call His name JESUS. "He will be great, and will be called*

the Son of the Highest; and the Lord God will give Him the throne of His father David. "And He will reign over the house of Jacob forever, and of His kingdom there will be no end." (Luke 1:26-33)

Angels are different than humans. One of their functions is to be messengers for God. Angels only say what they are told to say. Gabriel did not decide to say these things to Mary on his own. When Gabriel came to Mary, he brought her the living, powerful word of God. Mary listened to what Gabriel said, but she did not understand how it could happen.

Then Mary said to the angel, "How can this be, since I do not know a man?" (Luke 1:34)

Mary did not question the possibility of conceiving a child. She just wanted an explanation of how it could happen. Gabriel answered her question.

And the angel answered and said to her, "The Holy Spirit will come upon you, and the power of the Highest will overshadow you; therefore, also, that Holy One who is to be born will be called the Son of God. (Luke 1:35)

The explanation fits our previous discussion of the power of the word of God. Gabriel brought her the word of God concerning conceiving a child. The power within the word of God and the power of the Holy Spirit will cause the word to accomplish what it was sent forth to accomplish. But Mary had a part to play. To understand her part we have to understand the truth about faith.

So then faith comes by hearing, and hearing by the word of God. (Romans 10:17)

The Greek word translated "word" in this Scripture is "rhema." This word refers to God's spoken word as in a personally revealed word from God. Just hearing God's word will not produce faith in your heart. You have to receive that word as a word spoken from God to you. I grew up attending a church where my mother played the piano. I sat on the front pew in front of the piano as a child. I heard the gospel message many times before I was saved. I believed in God. I knew Jesus died for all the sinners in the world. But I was not saved just because I believed those things were true. One night I was in church for a revival service. The evangelist preached the same gospel message I had heard before. But something changed that night. The message penetrated my heart for the first time. My understanding about Jesus changed. The word became a "rhema," a personally revealed word to me. I realized that "I" was a sinner. I realized that Jesus died for "my" sins and that "I" needed a Savior. It was no longer that Jesus died for the world. He died for "me." I responded to the invitation that night to receive Jesus as my Savior. Faith arose in my heart. The seed of the word of God was manifested in my spirit and I was born again.

> *having been born again, not of corruptible seed but incorruptible, through the word of God which lives and abides forever, (1 Peter 1:23)*

Gabriel explained this same truth to Mary.

> *"For with God nothing will be impossible." (Luke 1:37)*

The original Greek text translated "nothing" is actually two words – "no rhema." The angel said, "with God no rhema will be impossible of being fulfilled." The Amplified Bible renders it this way:

> *For with God nothing is ever impossible and no word from God shall be without power or impossible of fulfillment. (Luke 1:37)(AMP)*

Stand back and look at this moment in history. Mankind is hopelessly lost in sin. Every person born is infected with the disease of sin. Once people sin, they become slaves to Satan, the ruler of the world system. Since God gave the authority on the Earth to man and man gave it to Satan, God had to use a man to get the authority back. But He could not use a sinful man because a sinful man is under the authority of Satan. God promised that the "Seed of the woman" would take back Satan's authority. When a man and a woman come together in sexual union, a child is conceived. But the woman produces the egg, not the seed. So how can there be a "Seed of the woman?" What did Gabriel deliver to the Virgin Mary? He delivered the word of God. Jesus said the word of God is a "seed" which contains God's life. God spoke through Isaiah that the word of God has power within it to perform what it was sent to perform. The "Seed of the woman" is the word of God which Gabriel delivered to Mary. All of creation was silent as Mary pondered what she had heard. The word which Gabriel delivered would not come to pass unless it became a "rhema" to Mary. She had to receive it as a word personally spoken and revealed to her.

> *Then Mary said, "Behold the maidservant of the Lord! Let it be to me according to your word." And the angel departed from her. (Luke 1:38)*

Mary agreed with God's word! She used the word "rhema" when she said, "Let it be to me according to your "**word**." When she believed the living, powerful word of God, the Holy Spirit overshadowed her just like the Holy Spirit caused God's word to be manifested in the beginning when God spoke the worlds into existence. Mary believed the word in her heart and the Holy Spirit caused the word to be manifested physically in her womb. Mary conceived the Son of God with the seed of God's word just as John described.

> *And the Word became flesh and dwelt among us, and we beheld His glory, the glory as of the only begotten of the Father, full of grace and truth. (John 1:14)*

Isaiah's prophecy came to pass. A virgin conceived by being impregnated with the living word of God. God made an entrance into the Earth as a man, but without being infected with sin! His father was God, not a sinful man. "God with us" or "Immanuel" became a reality. After Mary believed the word, Gabriel's mission was completed and he left. There had not been a human being on the Earth without sin since Adam and Eve. This is what made Jesus able to do the amazing things we will discuss in the next chapter.

CHAPTER 6

THE AUTHORITY OF JESUS

Imagine Jesus living in Heaven. He is with God, the Father. He has no opposition. He is clothed with the glory of God. He has all the divine attributes that come with being God. He has no spiritual, emotional, mental or physical limitations. And yet, all is not right with Jesus. He sees an Earth populated with people infected with sin. He sees people controlled by the Devil, in bondage to sin and the corruption of the world. He knows that people have no way to gain victory over the forces of darkness. So what must be done? Someone must take back the authority Satan seized from Adam. Since God gave that authority to a man, a human being must take it back. It must be a human being who is not subject to Satan because of sin. Jesus is going to have to come to Earth as a man to free people from the effects of sin. In order to function as a man, Jesus will have to willingly lay aside all His divine attributes.

Let this mind be in you which was also in Christ Jesus, who, being in the form of God, did not consider it robbery to be equal with God, but made Himself of no reputation, taking the form of a bond-servant, and coming in the likeness of men. And being found in appearance as a man, He humbled Himself and became obedient to the point of death, even the death of the cross. (Philippians 2:5-8)

Jesus is God. He has always been God and always will be God. When He came to the Earth as a human, He did not stop being God. He did, however, <u>lay aside</u> all His divine attributes to function as a man. In the Scripture cited above, the Greek word translated as the phrase, "made Himself of no reputation" is "kenoo," which means "to empty, evacuate, become nothing, to divest one's self of native dignity and power, to descend to an inferior position or condition." Remember, Jesus never stopped being God, but He did stop functioning as God to take on the form of a human and subject Himself to human weaknesses. The Amplified Bible gives a more thorough rendering of this passage of Scripture. This will help you see the full meaning of what Jesus did when He came to the Earth as a human.

> *Let this same attitude and purpose and [humble] mind be in you which was in Christ Jesus: [Let Him be your example in humility:] Who, although being essentially one with God and in the form of God [possessing the fullness of the attributes which make God God], did not think this equality with God was a thing to be eagerly grasped or retained, But stripped Himself [of all privileges and rightful dignity], so as to assume the guise of a servant (slave), in that He became like men and was born a human being. And after He had appeared in human form, He abased and humbled Himself [still further] and carried His obedience to the extreme of death, even the death of the cross! (Philippians 2:5-8)(AMP)*

Imagine Jesus in Heaven wearing a robe. The robe represents His divine glory, privileges, dignity and attributes. Jesus knows the only way to defeat Satan and give mankind an opportunity for victory over sin is to become a human being. Jesus willingly humbles Himself by stripping off the robe and laying it aside to become a human being. He could have held on tight to retain all His glory, but He didn't. By taking off that robe, He took on the limitations of humanity. He would get physically tired and have to rest and sleep. He would now have to eat to survive. He would be tempted to sin like every human being. He would have to make choices to align His will with the Father's will.

> *Now Jacob's well was there. Jesus therefore, <u>being wearied</u> from His journey, sat thus by the well... (John 4:6)*

> *But as they sailed <u>He fell asleep</u>... (Luke 8:23)*

> *Now it happened, as He went into the house of one of the rulers of the Pharisees <u>to eat bread</u> on the Sabbath, that they watched Him closely. (Luke 14:1)*

> *For we do not have a High Priest who cannot sympathize with our weaknesses, but <u>was in all points tempted as we are</u>, yet without sin. (Hebrews 4:15)*

> *...He knelt down and prayed, saying, "Father, if it is Your will, take this cup away from Me; nevertheless <u>not My will, but Yours, be done</u>." (Luke 22:41-42)*

Jesus didn't just borrow a human body, He <u>became</u> a human. He didn't have to do it. <u>He did it all for you and me to be free.</u> Life on Earth as a human was vastly different than life as God with all the divine attributes. Near the end of Jesus' time on Earth as a human, He talked to His Heavenly Father about regaining the glory He left behind.

> *Jesus spoke these words, lifted up His eyes to heaven, and said: "Father, the hour has come. Glorify Your Son, that Your Son also may glorify You, "as You have given Him authority over all flesh, that He should give eternal life to as many as You have given Him. "And this is eternal life, that they may know You, the only true God, and Jesus Christ whom You have sent. "I have glorified You on the earth. I have finished the work which You*

have given Me to do. "And now, O Father, glorify Me together with Yourself, with the glory which I had with You before the world was. (John 17:1-5)

I once spent three weeks in Jakarta, Indonesia on a ministry trip. Jakarta is a modern city in many ways, but the culture of Indonesia is different than America. At the end of my three weeks, I was ready to return home. I was ready to get away from all the mosquitoes. I no longer wanted to share my bedroom with a gecko, even though he ate mosquitoes. I was ready to use American-style bathroom and shower facilities. I was ready to eat American food. It was only three weeks, but I wanted to return to what I considered "normal."

Jesus had spent approximately 33 years away from His "normal" life in Heaven. He was looking forward to getting back. Notice He talked about *"the glory which I had with You before the world was."* He was ready to gain back the "glory" which He laid aside when He left Heaven to rescue mankind from sin and the Devil.

SATAN'S FOOTHOLD

Jesus lived on the Earth as a human being, but He was different from others in one very important aspect. Jesus was not infected with sin. Jesus never sinned. Sin is what caused Satan (the author of sin and death) to have authority (or reign) in sinner's lives.

For if by the one man's offense death reigned through the one, much more those who receive abundance of grace and of the gift of righteousness will reign in life through the One, Jesus Christ. (Romans 5:17)

Jesus referred to this important difference one day when He talked about His attitude toward the Devil, Satan, the ruler of the world system.

"I will no longer talk much with you, for the ruler of this world is coming, and he has nothing in Me. (John 14.30)

70

What did Jesus mean by this statement? We already established that Satan was referred to as the "ruler of this world." What gave Satan authority over people? Sin is what gave Satan authority over people. However, when Satan came around Jesus, since Jesus had no sin in Him, He could say about the Devil, *"he has nothing in Me."* Sin was in everyone else and sin gave Satan authority over everyone else. Satan's foothold to control people was their sin. But there was no sin in Jesus, nothing in Him that would give Satan authority to control Jesus. Satan had not seen a person without sin since the days of Adam.

> *And so it is written, "The first man Adam became a living being." The last Adam became a life-giving spirit. (1 Corinthians 15:45)*

The "last Adam" was Jesus. He was like Adam in the sense that He was without sin as Adam was in the beginning. Remember that Adam had authority over Satan until the day Adam sinned. Sin is what caused Adam to become a slave to sin and Satan. Sin is what caused Adam to die spiritually and then physically. If Adam had never sinned, he would still be living on Earth today. Since Jesus was without sin, He was immune from physical death until He chose to lay down His life as a sacrifice for all of mankind. A good example of this is when Jesus preached His first sermon in the Jewish synagogue. He told them He was the fulfillment of the Scripture He had just read from the prophet Isaiah.

> *So all those in the synagogue, when they heard these things, were filled with wrath, and rose up and thrust Him out of the city; and they led Him to the brow of the hill on which their city was built, that they might throw Him down over the cliff. Then passing through the midst of them, He went His way. (Luke 4:28-30)*

A crowd of people took Jesus out to a cliff to kill him. But what happened? He passed through the midst of them! Why was He able to do that? He walked away unharmed because it wasn't time for Him to die. He had no sin. He could not be killed until He chose to die. Look at two other examples of people unable to harm Jesus. They could not harm Him because He had no sin. He could not suffer death until it was time for Him to lay down His life.

> *Therefore they sought to take Him; but no one laid a hand on Him, because His hour had not yet come. (John 7:30)*

> *These words Jesus spoke in the treasury, as He taught in the temple; and no one laid hands on Him, for His hour had not yet come. (John 8:20)*

Jesus made it very clear to His followers that He would be the one to decide when He would die. Nobody would be able to decide that for Him.

> *"Therefore My Father loves Me, because I lay down My life that I may take it again. "No one takes it from Me, but I lay it down of Myself. I have power to lay it down, and I have power to take it again. This command I have received from My Father." (John 10:17-18)*

DEMONS WERE CONFUSED

If you ask a group of people how Jesus was able to do the miraculous things He did during His time on the Earth, most would answer, "Because He is God." But is that really correct? Did Jesus exercise authority over demons, have divine revelations and do miracles because He was God? If you answered "yes" to that question I encourage you to consider another viewpoint.

We discovered in the beginning of this chapter that Jesus laid down the powers that come with being God to assume the form of a human. It seems that Jesus <u>functioned</u> on the Earth as <u>a man (a human being) without sin</u> instead of as God. Now don't get upset with me about this. I already said that Jesus never stopped being God, even when He was on the Earth as a human. I am not suggesting that Jesus wasn't God or that He stopped being God. I am saying that, since He laid down the powers that come with being God to become a human, He must have been able to do what He did for some other reason. If this confuses you for a moment, let me show you some examples of demons being confused over the same issue.

> *Then they went into Capernaum, and immediately on the Sabbath He entered the synagogue and taught. And they were astonished at His teaching, for He taught them as one having authority, and not as the scribes. Now there was a man in their synagogue with an unclean spirit. And he cried out, saying, "Let us alone! What have we to do with You, Jesus of Nazareth? Did You come to destroy us? I know who You are—the Holy One of God!" (Mark 1:21-24)*

An unclean spirit is a demon spirit. Since demons are spirits, they operate in the spirit realm. The spirit realm is just as real as the physical world we can perceive with our physical senses. Several demon spirits were in control of the man in the synagogue (notice the demon said *"What have we to do with you"*). The demon used the man's voice to talk to Jesus. In the spirit realm, these demon spirits recognized Jesus as the Son of God. Demons were not evil when they were originally created by Jesus. Demons are a corrupted form of their original creation. Since Jesus created them, even in their now-corrupted state, they recognized their Creator as God, not as a human.

> *For by Him all things were created that are in heaven and that are on earth, visible and invisible, whether thrones or dominions or principalities or powers. All things were created through Him and for Him (Colossians 1:16)*

Jesus quickly dealt with the unclean spirit that was tormenting this man. He exercised the same authority over the demon spirit that Adam could have exercised over Satan in the Garden of Eden if he had made that choice.

> *But Jesus rebuked him, saying, "Be quiet, and come out of him!" And when the unclean spirit had convulsed him and cried out with a loud voice, he came out of him. Then they were all amazed, so that they questioned among themselves, saying, "What is this? What new doctrine is this? For with authority He commands even the unclean spirits, and they obey Him." (Mark 1:25-27)*

Now let's look at an example where the demons express their frustration and confusion at being controlled by Jesus.

> *When He had come to the other side, to the country of the Gergesenes, there met Him two demon-possessed men, coming out of the tombs, exceedingly fierce, so that no one could pass that way. And suddenly they cried out, saying, "What have we to do with You, Jesus, You Son of God? Have You come here to torment us before the time?" (Matthew 8:28-29)*

Once again, the demons operate in the spirit realm and recognize Jesus in the spirit as the Son of God. Then they ask a very interesting question. *"Have You come here to torment us before the time?"* These demons are concerned about being tormented and they talk about a certain time when their torment will occur. But they say that time of torment isn't here yet. What are they talking about? The answer is found in the Revelation given to John about the end of the Earth as we know it.

> *Now I saw a new heaven and a new earth, for the first heaven and the first earth had passed away. Also there was no more sea. Then I, John, saw*

> *the holy city, New Jerusalem, coming down out of heaven from God, prepared as a bride adorned for her husband. And I heard a loud voice from heaven saying, "Behold, the tabernacle of God is with men, and He will dwell with them, and they shall be His people. God Himself will be with them and be their God. (Revelation 21:1-3)*

One day we will have a new Heaven and a new Earth. But before that happens, Satan, his associates and his demons face a terrifying conclusion to their reign of terror on this Earth.

> *Then I saw an angel coming down from heaven, having the key to the bottomless pit and a great chain in his hand. He laid hold of the dragon, that serpent of old, who is the Devil and Satan, and bound him for a thousand years; and he cast him into the bottomless pit, and shut him up, and set a seal on him, so that he should deceive the nations no more till the thousand years were finished. But after these things he must be released for a little while.*
>
> *And I saw thrones, and they sat on them, and judgment was committed to them. Then I saw the souls of those who had been beheaded for their witness to Jesus and for the word of God, who had not worshiped the beast or his image, and had not received his mark on their foreheads or on their hands. And they lived and reigned with Christ for a thousand years. But the rest of the dead did not live again until the thousand years were finished. This is the first resurrection. Blessed and holy is he who has part in the first resurrection. Over such the second death has no power, but they shall be priests of God and of Christ, and shall reign with Him a thousand years. Now when the thousand years have expired, Satan will be released from his prison and will go out to deceive the nations which are in the*

> *four corners of the earth, Gog and Magog, to gather*
> *them together to battle, whose number is as the sand*
> *of the sea. They went up on the breadth of the earth*
> *and surrounded the camp of the saints and the*
> *beloved city. And fire came down from God out of*
> *heaven and devoured them. The devil, who deceived*
> *them, was cast into the lake of fire and brimstone*
> *where the beast and the false prophet are. <u>And they</u>*
> *<u>will be tormented day and night forever and ever</u>.*
> *(Revelation 20:1-10)*

Satan and his demons know a day of torment is coming. They know that God will execute this final horrible judgment of torment on them. These demons see Jesus in the spirit realm and they know He is God. They do not understand his authority. They are confused and are asking if He is exercising this final authority over them as God to send them to their eternity of torment. They asked Jesus, *"Have You come here to torment us <u>before the time</u>?"* They were challenging Jesus' authority over them. In other words, they were saying, "I know our time of torment is coming, but that time is not here yet. We know you are God and it is not time for God to send us to our place of torment." The demons thought Jesus was exercising His authority as God. But He was simply exercising His authority as "a man without sin." He was still God, but He wasn't using His authority as God. The reason He could tell the demons to leave the man was because He was "a man without sin." Here is a third example. This is Mark's account of the same event we looked at in Matthew 8.

> *Then they came to the other side of the sea, to the*
> *country of the Gadarenes. And when He had come*
> *out of the boat, immediately there met Him out of*
> *the tombs a man with an unclean spirit, who had*
> *his dwelling among the tombs; and no one could*
> *bind him, not even with chains, because he had*
> *often been bound with shackles and chains. And*
> *the chains had been pulled apart by him, and the*
> *shackles broken in pieces; neither could anyone*

tame him. And always, night and day, he was in the mountains and in the tombs, crying out and cutting himself with stones. When he saw Jesus from afar, he ran and worshiped Him. And he cried out with a loud voice and said, "What have I to do with You, Jesus, Son of the Most High God? <u>I implore You by God that You do not torment me.</u>" (Mark 5:1-7)

This demon was also confused. Like the others we looked at, he knew he was dealing with the Son of God. He thought he would not have to deal with God until the end of the age. So he used an incredible ploy to try to avoid the torment he thought was coming. He actually called on God for help! He was saying to God that it wasn't fair for Jesus to pick on him. The demon asked God to make Jesus leave him alone! He was confused. He thought Jesus was dealing with him as God. But Jesus was exercising His authority as a "man without sin."

Think about this. Jesus was able to tell demons to leave because Satan had "nothing in Him" – no sin in Him. <u>That means if we could get in the same shape, we could have the same authority over the Devil and demons</u>. But how could we do that? We have all sinned. What happens when a person is "born again?" That person's sin is removed! If your sin is removed, you have "nothing in you" that would give the Devil authority over you. It is really very simple.

1. SIN GIVES THE DEVIL AUTHORITY OVER YOU.

2. REMOVE THE SIN AND THE DEVIL HAS NO AUTHORITY OVER YOU.

3. JESUS IS THE ONLY ONE WHO CAN REMOVE YOUR SIN.

Isn't it wonderful what Jesus did for us? He made it possible to remove the sin that puts a person in bondage to the Devil! When you put your trust in Jesus for your salvation for the first time, you become a "new creation." All your sin is gone.

Therefore, if anyone is in Christ, he is a new creation; old things have passed away; behold, all things have become new. (2 Corinthians 5:17)

Sin is still a part of our lives, however, even after we are born again. Unfortunately, we all make mistakes and sin. Sin puts us back in a position of being under Satan's authority. So what do we do?

If we confess our sins, He is faithful and just to forgive us our sins and to cleanse us from all unrighteousness. (1 John 1:9)

When you sin, immediately confess your sin and receive God's forgiveness. Living in a state of unconfessed sin puts you in Satan's territory. Don't stay in the danger zone of unconfessed sin. Would you wade into the ocean during a hurricane warning? Would you climb on top of your house with tornado sirens wailing? You would not do those things because you know there is danger there. God already knows what you did wrong. You are not going to surprise Him when you confess your sin. He is waiting on you to admit your mistake so He can forgive you. Repent and confess your sin, receive forgiveness and get out from under Satan's control!

COOPERATING WITH GOD

Jesus cooperated with God. He obeyed God in every way. He knew when it was time for Him to lay down His life. Jesus went with His disciples to the Garden of Gethsemane to pray. Jesus struggled mightily with the thought of being betrayed and scourged and crucified. He knew He would suffer horribly. He even asked God if there was an alternative solution. After Jesus had prayed and confirmed with God that there was no other way to accomplish His mission, He was ready to "lay down His life."

Then they came to a place which was named Gethsemane; and He said to His disciples, "Sit here while I pray." And He took Peter, James, and

John with Him, and He began to be troubled and deeply distressed. Then He said to them, "My soul is exceedingly sorrowful, even to death. Stay here and watch." He went a little farther, and fell on the ground, and prayed that if it were possible, the hour might pass from Him. And He said, "Abba, Father, all things are possible for You. Take this cup away from Me; nevertheless, not what I will, but what You will." Then He came and found them sleeping, and said to Peter, "Simon, are you sleeping? Could you not watch one hour? "Watch and pray, lest you enter into temptation. The spirit indeed is willing, but the flesh is weak." Again He went away and prayed, and spoke the same words. And when He returned, He found them asleep again, for their eyes were heavy; and they did not know what to answer Him. Then He came the third time and said to them, "Are you still sleeping and resting? It is enough! <u>The hour has come; behold, the Son of Man is being betrayed into the hands of sinners</u>. "Rise, let us be going. See, My betrayer is at hand." And immediately, while He was still speaking, Judas, one of the twelve, with a great multitude with swords and clubs, came from the chief priests and the scribes and the elders. Now His betrayer had given them a signal, saying, "Whomever I kiss, He is the One; seize Him and lead Him away safely." As soon as He had come, immediately he went up to Him and said to Him, "Rabbi, Rabbi!" and kissed Him. Then they laid their hands on Him and took Him. And one of those who stood by drew his sword and struck the servant of the high priest, and cut off his ear. Then Jesus answered and said to them, "Have you come out, as against a robber, with swords and clubs to take Me? "I was daily with you in the temple teaching, and you did not seize Me. <u>But the Scriptures must be fulfilled</u>." (Mark 14:32-49)

Remember the other times people had tried to harm Jesus and they were unable to do so? Now, however, it is God's perfect time. Jesus allows Himself to be arrested, knowing this scenario will end with His death on the cross. He cooperated with God to complete the plan to rescue people from the effects of their sin.

AUTHORITY AND POWER

Jesus operated with both authority and power over the Devil and demons. Authority is different than power. Two different Greek words are used to describe power and authority. The Greek word used to describe "authority" is "exousia." It is translated as both "authority" and "power." Authority differs from power in this way. A police officer can stand in the middle of the street, hold up his hand and stop a huge dump truck full of concrete blocks. He doesn't do this because of his "power." He certainly isn't strong enough to physically stop the truck. He stops the truck because of the "authority" invested in him by the city where he serves as a police officer. Jesus operated in "exousia-authority." This book is focused on the "authority" given to the believer because of Jesus. Your <u>authority</u> is based on what Jesus accomplished on the cross.

> *Then they were all amazed, so that they questioned among themselves, saying, "What is this? What new doctrine is this? For with <u>authority</u> He commands even the unclean spirits, and they obey Him." (Mark 1:27)*

The Greek word "dunamis" is used to express the idea of "power." It is the root from which we get the words "dynamo" and "dynamite." It is translated in different places as "power, mighty works, and miracles." Jesus needed to walk in this power since He laid aside His powers of deity to become a human being.

> *Then Jesus returned in the <u>power</u> of the Spirit to Galilee, and news of Him went out through all the surrounding region. (Luke 4:14)*

This word is also used to refer to the same Holy Spirit power that was made available to all believers beginning on the day of Pentecost. Jesus described it this way:

> *"But you shall receive <u>power</u> when the Holy Spirit has come upon you; and you shall be witnesses to Me in Jerusalem, and in all Judea and Samaria, and to the end of the earth." (Acts 1:8)*

You and I need to learn to depend on the power of the Holy Spirit just like Jesus did. Jesus learned to flow in the power of the Holy Spirit to do mighty miracles through Him. Jesus was the Son of God for His entire existence on the Earth. He was the Son of God when He was ten years old. He was the Son of God when He was 20 years old. But we have no record of Jesus doing any miracles until after a very significant event in His life. Jesus' cousin, John the Baptist, was preaching a message of repentance and baptizing people in the Jordan River. One day Jesus made His way to the river to be baptized by John.

> *Then Jesus came from Galilee to John at the Jordan to be baptized by him. And John tried to prevent Him, saying, "I need to be baptized by You, and are You coming to me?" But Jesus answered and said to him, "Permit it to be so now, for thus it is fitting for us to fulfill all righteousness." Then he allowed Him. When He had been baptized, Jesus came up immediately from the water; and behold, the heavens were opened to Him, and He saw the Spirit of God descending like a dove and alighting upon Him. And suddenly a voice came from heaven, saying, "This is My beloved Son, in whom I am well pleased." (Matthew 3:13-17)*

Jesus received the power of the Holy Spirit when He came up out of the water. Now if Jesus was God, why did He need the power of the Holy Spirit? Because Jesus laid down His powers of deity when He came to the Earth and assumed the form of a man. That is why I can suggest to you that Jesus did not do miracles because He was God. Jesus did miracles because He was a man without sin, empowered by the Holy Spirit. One day Peter preached a magnificent sermon about Jesus to a man named Cornelius and a group of his relatives and friends. Peter made it clear during that sermon that Jesus operated under God's anointing of the power of the Holy Spirit.

> *"how God anointed Jesus of Nazareth with the Holy Spirit and with power, who went about doing good and healing all who were oppressed by the devil, for God was with Him. (Acts 10:38)*

Notice that Jesus was anointed *"with the Holy Spirit and with power."* Notice also that *"God was with Him."* Since Jesus was and is God, why did God have to be *"with Him?"* If Jesus did all His miracles because He was already God, then why did He need the power of the Holy Spirit and for God to be with Him? <u>Because Jesus operated on the Earth as a man without sin and anointed by the Holy Spirit</u>. When you understand this truth, then the next Scriptures will make more sense to you. Jesus explained to the disciples that He was the only way to God and that He and His Father were in total unity.

> *Jesus said to him, "I am the way, the truth, and the life. No one comes to the Father except through Me. "If you had known Me, you would have known My Father also; and from now on you know Him and have seen Him." (John 14:6-7)*

Philip was confused when Jesus made this statement. Jesus explained that He always demonstrated God's will with His life.

> *Philip said to Him, "Lord, show us the Father, and it is sufficient for us." Jesus said to him, "Have I been with you so long, and yet you have not known Me, Philip? He who has seen Me has seen the Father; so how can you say, 'Show us the Father'?*

> *"Do you not believe that I am in the Father, and the*
> *Father in Me? The words that I speak to you I do*
> *not speak on My own authority; but the Father who*
> *dwells in Me does the works. "Believe Me that I am*
> *in the Father and the Father in Me, or else believe*
> *Me for the sake of the works themselves.*
>
> *"Most assuredly, I say to you, he who believes in*
> *Me, the works that I do he will do also; and greater*
> *works than these he will do, because I go to My*
> *Father. (John 14:8-12)*

Jesus said *"the Father who dwells in Me does the works."* How did the Father dwell in Jesus? He dwelt in Him in the person of the Holy Spirit. Remember, Jesus needed the power of the Holy Spirit to operate on the Earth as a human being because He willingly laid down His powers of deity to become a man. Jesus was saying the Holy Spirit in Him did the miracles. Then Jesus said something truly amazing. He said *"he who believes in Me, the works that I do he will do also; and greater works than these he will do, because I go to My Father."* Do you believe in Jesus? Then Jesus said you would have the capability of doing the same miracles Jesus did and even greater miracles!

So, here is the question. If Jesus did His miracles because He was God, how can Jesus say you and I can do the same kinds of miracles? You and I will never become God. But, if Jesus did His miracles because He had the power of the Holy Spirit, then you and I have the <u>same</u> potential to do those <u>same</u> miracles if we have the <u>same</u> Holy Spirit living in us!

> *And I will pray the Father, and He will give you*
> *another Helper, that He may abide with you*
> *forever— "the Spirit of truth, whom the world*
> *cannot receive, because it neither sees Him nor*
> *knows Him; but you know Him, for He dwells with*
> *you and will be in you. (John 14:16-17)*

Jesus made it possible for sin to be removed from your life. With sin gone, the Holy Spirit can come and live inside you. The Holy Spirit is the same power source that Jesus used to do His miracles. And you can have that power source living in you! This means you have the potential to do mighty works. That does not mean you can do a miracle anytime you want to. Jesus could not even do that. Jesus turned water into wine – once. Jesus walked on water – once. Jesus put a man's ear back on his head after it had been cut off – once. Jesus fed a multitude of people with only a small amount of food – twice. My point is that you have the same potential for mighty works of the Holy Spirit, but God is the originator of miracles. You don't get to decide you are going to do a miracle and God has to make it happen. It is the other way around. If God wants to work a miracle through you, you need to cooperate with God to see it happen.

First, you need to be born again by putting your trust in Jesus for your salvation. Next, you need to ask Jesus to fill you with the Holy Spirit so you will have all the fullness of the power of God available to you. Then, learn to obey God by doing what He says in His word, the Bible, and by obeying His voice in your heart. Then you will see God work through you with the same power source, the Holy Spirit, Who was in Jesus. The power you need to resist sin, Satan and demons is based on what happened on the Day of Pentecost when Jesus sent the Holy Spirit into the Earth.

CHAPTER 7

FROM THE CROSS TO THE THRONE

Conquering sin and its devastating effects on humanity took a terrific toll on the human Jesus. Some things we can know about the process. Some things are not clearly explained in the Bible. I believe the Bible is God's revelation to man. If the Bible does not give us a full explanation of an event, I believe it is because we don't need to have all the details to walk with God. Now, through the revelation of the word of God, we are going to walk with Jesus through the amazing events that brought freedom from sin to us all.

> *Now they were on the road, going up to Jerusalem, and Jesus was going before them; and they were amazed. And as they followed they were afraid. Then He took the twelve aside again and began to tell them the things that would happen to Him: "Behold, we are going up to Jerusalem, and the Son of Man will be betrayed to the chief priests and to the scribes; and they will condemn Him to death and deliver Him to the Gentiles; "and they will mock Him, and scourge Him, and spit on Him, and kill Him. And the third day He will rise again." (Mark 10:32-34)*

Jesus knew the time to complete God's plan for man's salvation was near. The Holy Spirit had shown Him how it would play out. He gave His disciples advance warning of the things that would happen to Him. He did this so they would know these events were all part of God's plan.

> *But Jesus answered them, saying, "The hour has come that the Son of Man should be glorified. "Most assuredly, I say to you, unless a grain of wheat falls into the ground and dies, it remains alone; but if it dies, it produces much grain. "He who loves his life will lose it, and he who hates his life in this world will keep it for eternal life. "If anyone serves Me, let him follow Me; and where I am, there My servant will be also. If anyone serves Me, him My Father will honor. "Now My soul is troubled, and what shall I say? 'Father, save Me from this hour'? But for this purpose I came to this hour. "Father, glorify Your name." Then a voice came from heaven, saying, "I have both glorified it and will glorify it again." Therefore the people who stood by and heard it said that it had thundered. Others said, "An angel has spoken to Him." Jesus answered and said, "This voice did not come because of Me, but for your sake. "Now is the judgment of this world; now the ruler of this world will be cast out. "And I, if I am lifted up from the earth, will draw all peoples to Myself." This He said, signifying by what death He would die. (John 12:23-33)*

Jesus told them it was time for Him to be glorified. Remember, He laid down His glory to come to the Earth as a human. Now it is time for Him to get that glory back. Jesus said His soul (mental and emotional realm) was troubled. He knew the inconceivable physical and emotional pain that was coming. Yet He knew that was why He came to the Earth and He could not ask to be delivered from the necessity of this pain. Jesus tells them the time is now for Him to take the judgment for sin that the rest of us deserve. He said it was time for the ruler of this world (Satan) to be cast out of his position of authority over mankind. Then Jesus told them He would be lifted up (on a cross) to die and, therefore, draw people to Him as the solution to their sin problem.

Jesus had a meal with His disciples to demonstrate to them He was the final Passover Lamb that would take away the sin of the world. Then they went to a quiet place so Jesus could pray and prepare Himself for the physical, emotional and mental violence that was coming.

> *Coming out, He went to the Mount of Olives, as He was accustomed, and His disciples also followed Him. When He came to the place, He said to them, "Pray that you may not enter into temptation." And He was withdrawn from them about a stone's throw, and He knelt down and prayed, saying, "Father, if it is Your will, take this cup away from Me; nevertheless not My will, but Yours, be done." (Luke 22:39-42)*

Jesus asked one final time if there was any other way to accomplish His task. He made it clear He wanted God's will and not His own. That seems to indicate He could have chosen a different path than the one God had for Him. Jesus did exactly what He had taught His followers in *Matthew 6:10*. Jesus told the Father He wanted the Father's will to be accomplished, no matter the consequences to Him.

> *Then an angel appeared to Him from heaven, strengthening Him. And being in agony, He prayed more earnestly. Then His sweat became like great drops of blood falling down to the ground. (Luke 22:43-44)*

It is easy to gloss over this description of Jesus during His time of prayer. This was a monumental moment in human history as Jesus forced His will to stay in line with the Father's will. In a few hours, Jesus would experience the emotional devastation of seeing

His closest followers desert Him completely. He would see his close friend, Peter, deny that he even knows Jesus. He would hear people tell lies about Him to justify his execution. He would suffer excruciating pain when He is beaten, forced to carry His own cross and endure nails being driven into His hands and feet. He knows all this is about to happen.

Knowing something is coming and experiencing the event are two different things. I can remember when I became engaged to my wife. For a few months I was able to tell everyone, "I'm getting married." It sounded so exciting and fun! But then came the day of the wedding. My emotions and mental outlook changed. "My life is going to change radically," I thought. I realized I was making a lifetime commitment. As I dressed up in my white tuxedo, my emotions were in great turmoil. My engagement was about to end and the marriage would begin.

Jesus experienced the same type of thing, only on a magnitude beyond anything we can comprehend. He knew this was coming. He had described it to His disciples. But now He has to actually experience all of this. That is why an angel had to strengthen Him. That is why He is in such agony that He sweats blood due to the intense pressure He was feeling. He not only anticipates the pain I have already briefly described, but also the spiritual agony of His own Father turning away from Him as Jesus accepts the judgment for sin on our behalf.

I remember a time as a child when I became separated from my mother in a department store. I felt so alone. With my child's mind, I wondered if I would ever see her again. The store management called for my mother over the intercom. Shortly, she came to where I was waiting for her. I was so thrilled and relieved to be reunited with my mother! It had only been about 15 minutes, but to me it seemed like forever.

In all of eternity past, Jesus had never been separated from His Father. Even during His time as a human on Earth, He always had access to His Father. But now the time was coming when Jesus' Father would willingly turn away from Him. Part of the pressure Jesus was experiencing was the anticipation of this event. Eventually, however, after much prayer, Jesus was prepared to face the final episode of His life as a human on Earth. He had settled all the issues and was ready to complete God's plan. He rose, rejoined His sleepy disciples and told them the time had come.

> *Then He came the third time and said to them, "Are you still sleeping and resting? It is enough! The hour has come; behold, the Son of Man is being betrayed into the hands of sinners. (Mark 14:41-42)*

Jesus had told His disciples how He would be treated. He said He would be mocked. They probably never really understood his explanations, but Jesus wanted them to know in advance what would happen.

We move forward in the story to Jesus' arrival at His crucifixion site and the fulfillment of His words.

> *And when they had come to a place called Golgotha, that is to say, Place of a Skull, they gave Him sour wine mingled with gall to drink. But when He had tasted it, He would not drink. Then they crucified Him, and divided His garments, casting lots, that it might be fulfilled which was spoken by the prophet: "They divided My garments among them, And for My clothing they cast lots." Sitting down, they kept watch over Him there. And they put up over His head the accusation written against Him: THIS IS JESUS THE KING OF THE JEWS. Then two robbers were crucified with Him, one on the right and another on the left. And those who passed by blasphemed Him, wagging their heads and saying, "You who destroy the temple and build it in three days, save Yourself! If You are the Son of God, come down from the cross." Likewise the chief priests also, mocking with the scribes and elders, said, "He saved others; Himself He cannot save. If He is the King of Israel, let Him now come down from the cross, and we will believe Him. "He trusted in God;*

let Him deliver Him now if He will have Him; for He said, 'I am the Son of God.' " Even the robbers who were crucified with Him reviled Him with the same thing. (Matthew 27:33-44)

Jesus was mocked and ridiculed, just as He said. Suddenly, around noon, the Earth became eerily dark. The Jewish day began at sunrise. If we assume the sun rose around 6:00 a.m., the sixth hour of the day would have been around noon. The darkness remained for three hours. Darkness signifies the judgment of God. Remember when Satan originally rebelled against God and was cast down to the Earth? That is why darkness was on the face of the Earth until God put it back in order and brought the light as described in the first chapter of Genesis. Jesus was taking the judgment for sin upon Himself during this time of darkness.

Now from the sixth hour until the ninth hour there was darkness over all the land. (Matthew 27:45)

Jesus experienced at least three hours of agony on the cross. He endured the pain of suffering for our sins and then the reality of God, the Father, turning away from Him. This caused Him to cry out with the words originally found in **Psalm 22:1**.

And about the ninth hour Jesus cried out with a loud voice, saying, "Eli, Eli, lama sabachthani?" that is, "My God, My God, why have You forsaken Me?" (Matthew 27:46)

DID JESUS SIN?

Jesus cried out because He had never experienced the devastating effects of sin before. He had lived a perfect life with no sin. This is incredibly important to understand.

JESUS NEVER COMMITED SIN. <u>NEVER!</u>

I read a shocking statistic that 42% of American adults believe when Jesus Christ lived on Earth He committed sins.[1] Even among born-again Christians, 28% believe that statement is true![2] What is going on here? Are people really that ignorant about Jesus? Maybe you are one of those 42% or 28%. If so, I am so glad you are reading this book!

This is what happened to Jesus on the cross. I have added the names in parentheses to help clarify this Scripture.

> *For He (God) made <u>Him (Jesus) who knew no sin</u> to be sin for us, that we might become the righteousness of God in Him (Jesus). (2 Corinthians 5:21)*

There it is in perfect clarity. Jesus KNEW NO SIN. What happened on the cross was a GREAT EXCHANGE. Jesus was perfectly righteous. Righteousness means "right standing with God." Jesus was in perfect right-standing with God, the Father, because He never committed sin. All of mankind commits sin and is UNRIGHTEOUS because of our sinful acts. Jesus BECAME SIN <u>for us</u> when He hung on the cross. He DID NOT BECOME A SINNER. There is a big difference between the two. If Jesus had sinned during His life on Earth, He would have DESERVED to die. <u>He did not deserve to die because of His sin.</u> <u>He never sinned.</u> If Jesus deserved to die for His sins, He could not pay for my sins with His death. You and I deserve to die and be punished for our sins. But Jesus took care of that for us. **HE** took the punishment **WE** have earned for **OUR** sin and gave **US** the righteousness **HE** earned with **HIS** perfect life. What a deal! Now we can be in right standing with God as if we had never sinned. Not because we earned it, but because Jesus paid the penalty for sin and gave us the result of right-standing with God.

Some people have trouble saying they are "righteous." They equate righteousness with their own good works to earn it. You can't earn it. Righteousness is a gift that is received.

> *For if by the one man's offense death reigned through the one, much more those who <u>receive</u> abundance of grace and of <u>the gift of righteousness</u> will reign in life through the One, Jesus Christ.) (Romans 5:17)*

You can only be righteous because of what Jesus did for you. If Jesus can't make you righteous, what did He accomplish by dying on the cross? When you say you are righteous, you are bragging on what Jesus did, not on what you have done.

WHAT ABOUT THE OLD TESTAMENT LAW?

Jesus' life on Earth was drawing to a close. The agony of the cross would soon be over. Jesus fulfilled the commandment to honor His mother. He gave final instructions to John (who referred to himself as "the disciple whom He loved") to take care of His mother as if she were his own. Then Jesus died.

> *Now there stood by the cross of Jesus His mother, and His mother's sister, Mary the wife of Clopas, and Mary Magdalene. When Jesus therefore saw His mother, and the disciple whom He loved standing by, He said to His mother, "Woman, behold your son!" Then He said to the disciple, "Behold your mother!" And from that hour that disciple took her to his own home. After this, Jesus, knowing that all things were now accomplished, that the Scripture might be fulfilled, said, "I thirst!" Now a vessel full of sour wine was sitting there; and they filled a sponge with sour wine, put it on hyssop, and put it to His mouth. So when Jesus had received the sour wine, He said, "It is finished!" And bowing His head, He gave up His spirit. (John 19:25-30)*

What did Jesus mean when He said, "It is finished?" Was the plan of salvation complete? No, it wasn't complete. Jesus had to be raised from the dead to complete the plan. So what did He mean?

To further understand what happened, you must know about the Old Covenant law. Jesus initiated the beginning of a New Covenant. But the Old Covenant law first had to be fulfilled in Jesus as He describes below.

> *"Don't misunderstand why I have come. I did not come to abolish the law of Moses or the writings of the prophets. No, I came to fulfill them. I assure you, until heaven and earth disappear, even the smallest detail of God's law will remain until its purpose is achieved. (Matthew 5:17-18)(NLT)*

The Old Covenant required that blood be shed to atone for a person's sin. It only takes one sin to separate a person from God. Have you committed at least one sin in your life? Of course you have. We all have. Sin produces death (separation from God). We all were at one time "dead" spiritually and separated from God because of sin. But Jesus made a way for you to be made alive again by forgiving and removing your sin! You no longer have to comply with the Old Covenant requirements such as circumcision.

> *And you, being dead in your trespasses and the uncircumcision of your flesh, He has made alive together with Him, having forgiven you all trespasses, having wiped out the handwriting of requirements that was against us, which was contrary to us. And He has taken it out of the way, having nailed it to the cross. (Colossians 2:13-14)*

When a person commits a crime, he is charged with a certain offense. The charges are written out and a judge reads them at the time of a person's arraignment. The judge says you are charged with doing a certain thing and you can plead "guilty" or "not guilty." We are all guilty of sin. We all have a "rap sheet" which lists our offenses against God. If all our sins were listed on a piece of paper it would be like a *"handwriting of requirements that was against us, which was contrary to us."* If you told the truth, your answer to all the accusations of sins you have committed would be "guilty." When Jesus was nailed to the cross, He figuratively took your "rap sheet," your listing of sins you have committed, and He nailed it to the cross. It is as if He told the judge (God, the Father), "I am paying for this person's crimes against you. And since I am paying the penalty for this person, I am taking their record of sins away, never to be brought up again." He gave us <u>forgiveness</u> instead of <u>condemnation</u>, <u>life</u> instead of <u>death</u>.

The Old Covenant also required the High Priest of Israel to go into a place in the Jewish temple called the "Holy of Holies" once a year. This place was separated from the rest of the temple by a heavy, thick, tightly-woven curtain. The High Priest would cleanse himself appropriately according to the Old Covenant law and enter the Holy of Holies to present an animal blood sacrifice to cover over the sins of Israel for another year. A special manifestation of the presence of God was inside the Holy of Holies. Only the High Priest, after properly preparing himself, could enter this place. If he did not prepare himself correctly, he would die when he entered the Holy of Holies and experienced the presence of God. Sin cannot exist in the presence of God. It was as if there was a sign on this portion of the temple saying, "Keep out! You cannot experience God's presence with sin in your life."

> *And Jesus cried out again with a loud voice, and yielded up His spirit. Then, behold, the veil of the temple was torn in two from top to bottom; and the earth quaked, and the rocks were split, (Matthew 27:50-51)*

We know Jesus said, "It is finished," and died physically. Jesus was saying <u>the final blood sacrifice had been made</u>. The Old Covenant system of blood sacrifices was finished. There would <u>never again</u> be a need for the High Priest to go into the Holy of Holies to offer a blood sacrifice. Because of that, the heavy, thick veil that separated the Holy of Holies from the rest of the temple was supernaturally **"torn in two from top to bottom."** This also showed us that the presence of God was no longer limited to the Holy of Holies. Now, it is possible for every person who chooses to trust in Jesus to experience God's presence. Jesus' spirit was released from His body and the Earth quaked as Jesus' spirit descended into the heart of the Earth, into a place called Hades. Jesus told His disciples about this event earlier in His life.

> *Then some of the scribes and Pharisees answered, saying, "Teacher, we want to see a sign from You." But He answered and said to them, "An evil and adulterous generation seeks after a sign, and no sign will be given to it except the sign of the prophet Jonah. "For as Jonah was three days and three nights in the belly of the great fish, <u>so will the Son of Man be three days and three nights in the heart of the Earth</u>. (Matthew 12:38-40)*

Paul also describes this event in his letter to the Christians in Ephesus.

> *But to each one of us grace was given according to the measure of Christ's gift. Therefore He says: "When He ascended on high, He led captivity captive, And gave gifts to men." (Now this, "He ascended"—what does it mean but that <u>He also first descended into the lower parts of the earth</u>? He who descended is also the One who ascended far above all the heavens, that He might fill all things.) (Ephesians 4:7-10)*

Jesus eventually ascended (went up) to Heaven, but first he <u>descended</u> (went down) into the heart of the Earth. So where did He go and what did He do for those three days? I have read and heard many theories. All that really matters, though, is what the Bible says. Jesus told a story that gives us a glimpse into this hidden place called Hades.

"There was a certain rich man who was clothed in purple and fine linen and fared sumptuously every day. "But there was a certain beggar named Lazarus, full of sores, who was laid at his gate, "desiring to be fed with the crumbs which fell from the rich man's table. Moreover the dogs came and licked his sores. "So it was that the beggar died, and was carried by the angels to Abraham's bosom. The rich man also died and was buried. "And being in torments in Hades, he lifted up his eyes and saw Abraham afar off, and Lazarus in his bosom. "Then he cried and said, 'Father Abraham, have mercy on me, and send Lazarus that he may dip the tip of his finger in water and cool my tongue; for I am tormented in this flame.' "But Abraham said, 'Son, remember that in your lifetime you received your good things, and likewise Lazarus evil things; but now he is comforted and you are tormented. 'And besides all this, between us and you there is a great gulf fixed, so that those who want to pass from here to you cannot, nor can those from there pass to us.' (Luke 16:19-26)

Since Jesus referred to "*a certain rich man*" and a "*certain beggar named Lazarus,*" it seems this is a true story, rather than a fictional parable used to illustrate a point. We don't know the details of either of these men's lives, but we know the rich man died and went to a place of torment. The beggar named Lazarus went to the same place Abraham went when he died and where there was comfort instead of torment. Hades is the name for this holding place for all people who died under the Old Covenant before Jesus came to take away our sin. Since there can be no sin in Heaven, those who died before Jesus had to wait somewhere for Him to complete His work. Hades was the place for both those who trusted and lived for God and those who were wicked and had no time for God. There was a gulf between the two compartments, however, so people could see across the gulf. The wicked rich man called out to Abraham and asked for Lazarus to help relieve some of the agony of his torment. Abraham told the rich man the gulf between the two compartments could not be crossed and he was getting what he deserved for rejecting God while he was alive on the Earth.

When Jesus died on the cross, His spirit descended into Hades, in the heart of the Earth, to remain for three days. So, to which side did Jesus go? Did He go to the side of torment with the wicked or the side of comfort with those who trusted God? Does the Bible give us any answers?

Jesus was crucified between two criminals. One of the two admitted his sin and asked Jesus for help before he died. Jesus told him what would happen to him later that afternoon.

> *Then he said to Jesus, "Lord, remember me when You come into Your kingdom." And Jesus said to him, "Assuredly, I say to you, today you will be with Me in Paradise." (Luke 23:42-43)*

Jesus told the criminal he would be with Him "in Paradise." Which side of Hades would be described as "Paradise?" The side with Abraham and Lazarus would be a place of comfort and paradise. The Bible seems to say that Jesus went to the peaceful side, the good side. But Peter has something interesting to say in one of his letters to Christians.

> *For Christ also suffered once for sins, the just for the unjust, that He might bring us to God, being put to death in the flesh but made alive by the Spirit, by whom also <u>He went and preached to the spirits in prison, who formerly were disobedient</u>, when once the Divine longsuffering waited in the days of Noah, while the ark was being prepared, in which a few, that is, eight souls, were saved through water. (1 Peter 3:18-20)*

> *For this reason <u>the gospel was preached also to those who are dead</u>, that they might be judged*

according to men in the flesh, but live according to
God in the spirit. (1 Peter 4:6)

Which side of Hades would include the "disobedient" "in prison"? It would seem to be the side of torment, not paradise. Perhaps Jesus went to the torment side to tell them of the wonderful salvation that could have been theirs if they had only chosen to live for God instead of fulfilling their own selfish desires. "Those who are dead" could include both sides. Maybe Jesus went to the paradise side to tell them the good news that the Messiah they had been awaiting had come.

VICTORY OVER SIN, SATAN AND DEATH

We may never know exactly what went on in the heart of the Earth for those three days. If it were critical that we know all the details, I believe God would have provided them. But since He didn't, I am comfortable with this description of what happened after three days.

"People of Israel, listen! God publicly endorsed
Jesus of Nazareth by doing wonderful miracles,
wonders, and signs through him, as you well know.
But you followed God's prearranged plan. With the
help of lawless Gentiles, you nailed him to the cross
and murdered him. However, God released him
from the horrors of death and raised him back to
life again, for death could not keep him in its grip.
(Acts 2:22-24)(NLT)

Jesus was dead without just cause. He never sinned. He never deserved to die. He willingly suffered death and separation from God, the wages of sin, for you and me. Therefore, death could not hold Him. **After three days, God's mighty resurrection power raised Jesus up and thereby conquered death for all time!** He conquered Satan, the author of sin and death, by overcoming the grip of the grave and rising at His Father's command. **Whatever**

happened down there, it was enough to free us from the penalty of sin. That is all we need to know!

Jesus was accused of teaming up with the Devil at one time in His ministry. The crowds had a hard time understanding how He was able to cast demons out of people. So they made up their own explanation of what was happening. People still do that today. If they don't understand what is happening, they attribute it to the Devil to scare people away from experiencing the true power of God. Jesus took this opportunity to set them straight and reveal something very important about how He would soon defeat Satan for all of us.

> *And He was casting out a demon, and it was mute. So it was, when the demon had gone out, that the mute spoke; and the multitudes marveled. But some of them said, "He casts out demons by Beelzebub, the ruler of the demons." Others, testing Him, sought from Him a sign from heaven. But He, knowing their thoughts, said to them: "Every kingdom divided against itself is brought to desolation, and a house divided against a house falls. "If Satan also is divided against himself, how will his kingdom stand? Because you say I cast out demons by Beelzebub. "And if I cast out demons by Beelzebub, by whom do your sons cast them out? Therefore they will be your judges. "But if I cast out demons with the finger of God, surely the kingdom of God has come upon you. "When a strong man, fully armed, guards his own palace, his goods are in peace. "But when a stronger than he comes upon him and overcomes him, he takes from him all his armor in which he trusted, and divides his spoils. (Luke 11:14-22)*

Jesus said a lot in the last two sentences. Notice He is talking about exercising authority over the Devil. Satan and demons are the subjects of the discussion. Jesus didn't change the subject at the end. He was still on the same topic.

Gangs and thugs rule in some neighborhoods in America. Many times, there is one dude who is bigger, meaner and more intimidating than all the others. You know not to mess with this guy. He doesn't have to worry about someone stealing his stuff. Everyone knows if you take what belongs to him you are in big trouble. You may take what he has, but you will soon be dead because he is the meanest, strongest guy on his turf.

Jesus is describing Satan this way. Satan was stronger than anyone. He was fully armed with the authority given him by sinful mankind. His "goods" refers to the authority he had because of sin. Every human being was born infected with sin. Every human being would eventually sin and come under the authority of Satan. He was at peace. That is, until a stronger one showed up. Jesus is the "stronger one!" Remember, Jesus said that Satan "had nothing in him." There was no sin in Jesus. Sin is the basis for Satan's authority. Because Jesus was a man without sin, He was stronger than Satan. Jesus was able to go into Satan's territory of sickness and demonic control and demonstrate His authority by setting people free.

Jesus then describes what He would soon do to provide the same authority He had over the Devil to anyone willing to receive His gift of salvation. Jesus said the stronger one (Jesus) would overcome Satan and take away his "armor." Armor is the protection a soldier wears into battle. Satan was protected because of mankind's sin. Jesus said He would overcome the Devil and divide the "spoils." Spoils are what you take from a vanquished foe. If a king attacked another country and won the war, everything the defeated king owned would then belong to the victorious king. Jesus said He was stronger than Satan, would conquer the Devil and "divide" the spoils. One of the wonderful things about Jesus is that <u>He defeated Satan for you and me</u>. He didn't do it for Himself. Remember, in Heaven before He came to the Earth as a human, He had no problems with the Devil. Even when He walked the Earth, Jesus was always able to demonstrate authority over Satan. Jesus said He was going to take back the authority over mankind that Satan owned and "divide" it, or give it away. After Jesus completed His work on the cross and was resurrected, He gave His authority to all who receive Him as Savior and are cleansed of sin. <u>Sin gives the Devil authority</u>. <u>Jesus removed the sin so we could be free from Satan's domination</u>.

THE FINAL SACRIFICE

The book called Hebrews was written to Jewish people to help them understand how Jesus was the fulfillment of all the Old Covenant sacrifices required by the law. A more detailed look at how Jesus accomplished this will shed more light on how Jesus freed us from Satan's control. Chapter Nine of Hebrews describes the place I briefly spoke of earlier called the Holy of Holies.

> *Now when these things had been thus prepared, the priests always went into the first part of the taber-nacle, performing the services. But into the second part the high priest went alone once a year, not without blood, which he offered for himself and for the people's sins committed in ignorance; (Hebrews 9:6-7)*

All the priests could minister in the first part of the tabernacle, the outer area. But only the High Priest would go into the second part, the Holy of Holies, once a year. The High Priest would first offer a blood sacrifice for his own sins and then offer another blood sacrifice for the sins of the people.

> *the Holy Spirit indicating this, that the way into the Holiest of All was not yet made manifest while the first tabernacle was still standing. (Hebrews 9:8)*

The manifested presence of God was in the Holiest of All (the Holy of Holies behind the thick veil). As long as the tabernacle and veil were still standing, mankind could not readily enjoy God's presence. God was limited in expressing Himself because of man's sin.

> *It was symbolic for the present time in which both gifts and sacrifices are offered which cannot make*

> *him who performed the service perfect in regard to the conscience— concerned only with foods and drinks, various washings, and fleshly ordinances imposed until the time of reformation. (Hebrews 9:9-10)*

Under the Old Covenant, before Jesus, gifts and blood sacrifices were made to cover over sin. Eating certain foods and other outward rituals were important to find favor with God. However, those sacrifices and outer actions could never cleanse the conscience. It would be like having a stain on your living room carpet. If you put a coffee table over the stain, nobody will see the stain, but you will know it is still there. The stain is only covered up. However, if you clean the carpet and remove the stain, it is gone forever. You don't have to cover it with a coffee table anymore. Under the Old Covenant, sin could be covered over, but not removed. People would still have a guilty conscience because their sin was only covered, not removed.

> *But Christ came as High Priest of the good things to come, with the greater and more perfect tabernacle not made with hands, that is, not of this creation. (Hebrews 9:11)*

Jewish people did not want to let go of their High Priest. That office had been a part of their culture for hundreds of years. The writer of the book of Hebrews explains that Jesus is the final High Priest anyone will ever need. Jesus entered a tabernacle with a blood sacrifice, however, it was not one made by human hands.

> *Not with the blood of goats and calves, but with His own blood He entered the Most Holy Place once for all, having obtained eternal redemption. For if the blood of bulls and goats and the ashes of a heifer, sprinkling the unclean, sanctifies for the purifying of the flesh, how much more shall the blood of Christ, who through the eternal Spirit offered Himself without spot to God, cleanse your*

conscience from dead works to serve the living God? (Hebrews 9:12-14)

Jesus went into a different Holy of Holies (Most Holy Place) with His own blood. His blood did more than cover sin for another year. His blood was the Holy, sinless blood of God which was powerful enough to remove sin forever! His blood provided an eternal redemption and a <u>cleansing of the conscience</u>. Now you can be free from a guilty conscience! You can be free from the continual guilt of past sin.

Jesus was on His way to Heaven to complete His work when He spoke to Mary Magdalene at the empty tomb on resurrection morning.

> *Jesus said to her, Do not cling to Me [do not hold Me], for I have not yet ascended to the Father. But go to My brethren and tell them, I am ascending to My Father and your Father, and to My God and your God. (John 20:17)(AMP)*

Now we find out something truly amazing. The tabernacle on Earth, where the priests did their work and the High Priest would enter the Holy of Holies once a year, was a copy of the one in Heaven. Jesus acted on our behalf as our High Priest by entering the <u>Heavenly</u> presence of God in the <u>Heavenly</u> Holy of Holies to present His own sinless blood.

> *For Christ has not entered the holy places made with hands, which are copies of the true, but into Heaven itself, now to appear in the presence of God for us; not that He should offer Himself often, as the high priest enters the Most Holy Place every year with blood of another— He then would have had to suffer often since the foundation of the world; but now, once at the end of the ages, He has appeared to put away sin by the sacrifice of Himself. (Hebrews 9:24-26)*

The difference between the Earthly High Priest and Jesus as our High Priest is significant. Jesus only had to offer His blood once. He would not have to do it annually. Jesus appeared to "put away sin" or "remove it" rather than cover it over.

Because Jesus became one of us, a human being, He was able to pay the sin penalty and nullify the hold the Devil had on people. We no longer have to be afraid of Satan or afraid of physical death if we know Jesus as our Savior.

> *Because God's children are human beings—made of flesh and blood—Jesus also became flesh and blood by being born in human form. For only as a human being could he die, and only by dying could he break the power of the Devil, who had the power of death. (Hebrews 2:14)(NLT)*

Jesus now has control of Hades. Nobody has to go to a place of torment anymore. We all have a choice because Jesus has the keys, the authority. Satan can't make anyone go to Hades anymore because of their sin. Every person has an opportunity now to be free from sin and free from the control of the Devil.

> *I am He who lives, and was dead, and behold, I am alive forevermore. Amen. And I have the keys of Hades and of Death. (Revelation 1:18)*

When Jesus defeated Satan, he took away his most powerful weapon, sin. Now, Satan has to rely on deception and intimidation to control people. I made a team ministry trip to Ukraine one time. The last day we were there, after we finished our time of ministry, we took the opportunity to visit some sights in Kiev. I went into a World War II museum to look around. At one point in my tour, I came upon a display of a huge bomb which would have been dropped from a plane during the war. The bomb could have caused the death of everyone in the museum if it had detonated. But I wasn't afraid to stand next to the bomb because the bomb had been disarmed. I knew it could not harm me.

Jesus has disarmed Satan. In fact, Jesus publicly shamed Satan in the spirit realm when He defeated him by rising from the dead. You don't have to fear Satan. Jesus made it possible for you to be free from his control by removing your sin.

> *You were dead because of your sins and because your sinful nature was not yet cut away. Then God made you alive with Christ. He forgave all our sins. He canceled the record that contained the charges against us. He took it and destroyed it by nailing it to Christ's cross. In this way, <u>God disarmed the evil rulers and authorities</u>. He shamed them publicly by his victory over them on the cross of Christ. (Colossians 2:13-15)(NLT)*

Before Jesus came, Hades was a place where everyone's spirit went when they died. It was a place of two compartments. One of peace and tranquility, described as paradise. The other side was a place of torment for the wicked dead. The believers were only there temporarily. They were not in Heaven yet because their sin had not been removed. However, once Jesus paid for their sin, He took the righteous dead up to Heaven to enjoy the presence of God and all that God had prepared for them. They had been in captivity, waiting on Jesus to pay for their sins. Once that was accomplished, Jesus took them out of Hades and up to their final destination of Heaven.

> *Therefore He says: "When He ascended on high, He led captivity captive, And gave gifts to men." (Ephesians 4:8)*

The paradise side of Hades is now empty. All Old Testament believers are gone. Maybe it is full of cobwebs! Now when a Christian's body can no longer function on Earth and dies, his spirit goes straight to Heaven and into the presence of the Lord. No stop-overs in Hades are required.

So we are always confident, knowing that while we are at home in the body we are absent from the Lord. For we walk by faith, not by sight. We are confident, yes, well pleased rather <u>to be absent from the body and to be present with the Lord</u>. (2 Corinthians 5:6-8)

<u>Jesus did all this for us</u>. He gained this wonderful authority over Satan and gave it away to us. We now have authority to use His name as if He were here.

And Jesus came and spoke to them, saying, "All authority has been given to Me in heaven and on earth. (Matthew 28:18)

Sin can no longer control us. Jesus made a way for us to be totally free from the power of sin. Don't let the Devil fill your mind with thoughts that there are some sins you just can't overcome. That is a lie. <u>Jesus gave us complete victory over sin</u>. You can overcome lust, drug addiction, adultery, lying, homosexual behavior, anger and any other sin you can think of. We tell sin what to do, not the other way around.

And since we died with Christ, we know we will also share his new life. We are sure of this because Christ rose from the dead, and he will never die again. Death no longer has any power over him. He died once to defeat sin, and now he lives for the glory of God. So you should consider yourselves dead to sin and able to live for the glory of God through Christ Jesus. Do not let sin control the way you live; do not give in to its lustful desires. Do not let any part of your body become a tool of wickedness, to be used for sinning. Instead, give yourselves completely to God since you have been given new life. And use your whole body as a tool to do what is right for the glory of God. <u>Sin is no longer your master</u>, for

*you are no longer subject to the law, which enslaves
you to sin. Instead, you are free by God's grace.
(Romans 6:8-14)(NLT)*

---

[1] The Barna Group Website, 2005, Barna By Topic, Beliefs: Trinity, Satan, www.
barna.org, Ventura, CA

[2] The Barna Group Website, 2005, Barna By Topic, Beliefs: Born Again Christians,
www.barna.org, Ventura, CA

CHAPTER 8

THE TRUTH ABOUT DEMONS

I lived in Montgomery, Alabama for 12 years. During that time I was able to visit Maxwell Air Force Base and speak with the head of the "War Gaming" training department. He explained to me how the military trains its leaders through "war gaming" exercises. One team will assume the role of a potential enemy of the United States. The other team will practice their strategies as leaders of the United States military. The opposing team uses the tactics and methods of the country they are simulating. The U.S. team uses the tactics and methods of the United States military. The purpose of the "game" is to prepare to win a potential war or conflict of any kind with the enemy whose military forces we are simulating. In order for one team to replicate a potential enemy's tactics, they have to know something about how their enemy does battle. They have to understand their enemy's military logic and reasoning process. They have to have knowledge of how a potential enemy operates so they can successfully defeat them.

Satan is the enemy of every Christian. <u>You have no choice but to do battle with him</u>. As long as you live on this Earth, the Devil will be your enemy. Do you want to know how to defeat him? Then you have to understand his battlefield logic and methods of operation. God wants you to know the tactics of our enemy, Satan.

Now whom you forgive anything, I also forgive. For if indeed I have forgiven anything, I have forgiven that one for your sakes in the presence of Christ, <u>lest Satan should take advantage of us; for we are not ignorant of his devices.</u> (2 Corinthians 2:10-11)

To keep Satan from getting the advantage over us; for we are not ignorant of his wiles and intentions. (2 Corinthians 2:11)(AMP)

The word, "ignorant" means "without knowledge." God does not want us to go into battle with Satan without knowledge of his devices, schemes and methods of operation. If you don't know what to expect, Satan can take advantage of you. God does not want the Devil to take advantage of you. That is why He has exposed the schemes of the enemy in the Bible.

The Bible is clear that we should have nothing to do with the Devil or any of his works. God always has our best interests at heart when He gives us instructions about life. It is to our benefit to listen to God's advice and stay completely away from anything involving Satan. The old saying, "Don't play with fire unless you want to get burned" applies here. Don't willingly walk around in Satan's playground and play with his toys unless you want to get hurt.

For though your hearts were once full of darkness, now you are full of light from the Lord, and your behavior should show it! For this light within you produces only what is good and right and true. Try to find out what is pleasing to the Lord. <u>Take no part in the worthless deeds of evil and darkness;</u> instead, rebuke and expose them. It is shameful even to talk about the things that ungodly people do in secret. But when the light shines on them, it becomes clear how evil these things are. (Ephesians 5:8-13)(NLT)

Did you ever have a monster in your room when you were a child? Most of us imagined someone or something was in the closet or outside the window or under the bed. You may have been absolutely convinced it was a monster until your Mom or Dad turned the light on in your bedroom. Then what happened? The "monster" turned out to be your pants on the door or a tree limb outside your window or something like that. The light revealed the truth.

I am going to shine the light of God's word on the works of the Devil so you will be able to see the truth and avoid any kind of involvement with Satan. I am going to expose his works and the reality behind his deception. When I talk about Satan's works, your mind may run wild and think I will be describing extreme instances of demonic control. Your only frame of reference for understanding Satan may be a movie such as "The Exorcist" which depicted a demon-possessed head spinning, green vomit, a bed levitating and other paranormal events. These things do happen in extreme cases. I will focus, however, on the more subtle influences Satan can have in people's lives and how to recognize and avoid them.

DECEPTION IS SATAN'S FAVORITE TOOL. The Devil would like you to believe he does not even exist. If you don't think he exists, you won't resist him and he will have his way in your life. I read an amazing statistic that 60% of Americans believe, "Satan is not a living being but is a symbol of evil."[1] That means Satan can do anything he wants to 60% of Americans because they have no clue he is at work to disrupt their lives. Let me assure you, Satan is real and demons are real. I am not afraid of him, but I respect his ability to create problems for me and to do everything he can to stop me from fulfilling God's plans for my life.

WHERE DID DEMONS COME FROM?

The Bible isn't clear about the origin of demons. I have heard several theories and they all have some merit and can be marginally backed up with Scripture. The most common theory is that they are fallen angels. The Bible book we call "Revelation" is a record of the vision God gave to the Apostle John. The revelation uses vivid imagery to describe events. The Scripture passage below appears to describe the following broad range of historical events:

1. Satan's persuasion of a third of the angels to join him in his rebellion against God.
2. Satan's attempt to kill Jesus soon after He was born by motivating Herod to kill all the boys two years and under born in Bethlehem.
3. Jesus' birth as a human being.
4. Jesus' resurrection and ascension to the Father in Heaven.

And another sign appeared in heaven: behold, a great, fiery red dragon having seven heads and ten horns, and seven diadems on his heads. His tail drew a third of the stars of heaven and threw them to the earth. And the dragon stood before the woman who was ready to give birth, to devour her Child as soon as it was born. She bore a male Child who was to rule all nations with a rod of iron. And her Child was caught up to God and His throne. (Revelation 12:3-5)

That rebellion cost Lucifer his position of authority in Heaven and turned him into Satan, the enemy of all God's creation. Some people believe the angels who joined with Lucifer and became corrupted are what we now know as demons. That may be true. But the Bible also describes the fallen angels as being restrained in some way. We know that demons are still active in the world and are not held in a prison awaiting their judgment.

For if God did not spare the angels who sinned, but cast them down to hell and delivered them into chains of darkness, to be reserved for judgment; (2 Peter 2:4)

And the angels who did not keep their proper domain, but left their own abode, He has reserved in

> *everlasting chains under darkness for the judgment*
> *of the great day; (Jude 6)*

So where did demons come from? Are they fallen angels? I don't know for sure. Whatever they are, God originally created them as good and not evil. Wherever they came from, they became corrupted and are now the enemies of God and Christians. I know one thing for sure. Demons are not the spirits of dead people who come back to haunt you. If you think you "see dead people," you are seeing demons and not your Uncle Tony! Keep reading and I will show you why it doesn't concern me to know with certainty the details of their origins.

> *Beloved, do not believe every spirit, but test the spirits, whether they are of God; because many false prophets have gone out into the world. By this you know the Spirit of God: Every spirit that confesses that Jesus Christ has come in the flesh is of God, and every spirit that does not confess that Jesus Christ has come in the flesh is not of God. And this is the spirit of the Antichrist, which you have heard was coming, and is now already in the world. (1 John 4:1-3)*

Every religious leader in the world who professes to believe in God is not of God. You shouldn't believe everything someone says just because they claim to be speaking for God. For example, a man named Jim Jones founded a cult movement called The People's Temple and claimed to be speaking for God. Jones developed a belief in which he and his followers would all die together and move to another planet for a life of bliss. In 1978, he influenced over 900 people who followed him to Jonestown, Guyana, to drink poison and kill themselves. He was a deceiver. He was not speaking for God. His followers suffered the consequences of not "testing the spirit" that was in control of Jim Jones.

God gave us a test to determine if a person is really speaking on His behalf. Does this person believe that Jesus was God manifested in the flesh? Or does he think Jesus was only a good man with some wise sayings? Or he may believe Jesus was a prophet, but not God manifested in human form. Many cults can be exposed with this simple truth. Jehovah's Witnesses, for example, may come to your door and tell you they believe in Jesus. But when you ask if Jesus was God in human form, they will say they do not believe that to be true. If you are wondering if a person is in a cult, ask them what they believe about Jesus. The answer will help to reveal the spirit controlling that group of people.

You are of God, little children, and have overcome them, because He who is in you is greater than he who is in the world. (1 John 4:4)

This is why I don't lose any sleep trying to figure out where demons came from. It doesn't matter. Jesus defeated the Devil and gave me authority over Satan and all his demons. <u>If you are born again and free from sin, you have the same authority Jesus had over demons.</u> Jesus in me is greater than any demon in the world. That is why I do not fear the Devil or demons. Satan himself (the Devil) probably does not attempt to inhabit you or anyone you know. Demons under Satan's control are who we must learn to recognize and resist. In the context of this book, Satan and demons have the same tactics, and Christians have authority over both.

COUNTERFEITER

Satan does not have the same kind of creative power as God. So Satan tries to counterfeit what God has created. The Devil wants to deceive you into believing that his supernatural stunts are equal to God. He tries to take what is pure and holy and good and pervert it for his own purposes. Here is an example of Satan counterfeiting God's power. God had spoken to Moses to confront Pharaoh and tell him to release God's people from their slavery in Egypt. Moses' brother, Aaron, went with Moses to help him. God revealed to them He would perform a miracle to validate their claims that they were speaking on God's behalf.

> *Then the LORD spoke to Moses and Aaron, saying,*
> *"When Pharaoh speaks to you, saying, 'Show a*
> *miracle for yourselves,' then you shall say to Aaron,*
> *'Take your rod and cast it before Pharaoh, and let*
> *it become a serpent.' " So Moses and Aaron went*
> *in to Pharaoh, and they did so, just as the LORD*
> *commanded. And Aaron cast down his rod before*
> *Pharaoh and before his servants, and it became a*
> *serpent. But Pharaoh also called the wise men and*
> *the sorcerers; so the magicians of Egypt, they also*
> *did in like manner with their enchantments. For*
> *every man threw down his rod, and they became*
> *serpents. But Aaron's rod swallowed up their rods.*
> *(Exodus 7:8-12)*

Pharaoh's sorcerers seemed to have the same power of God. They appeared to duplicate God's miracle. But look at the last part of the last verse. *"But Aaron's rod swallowed up their rods."* God's power is always greater than Satan's power! The serpent God created swallowed up the Devil's substitute. Don't let the Devil fool you into thinking that his power and God's power are equal. In a battle between God and the Devil, God always wins. In a battle between a Christian and the Devil, the Christian should always win because we have God's delegated authority.

Satan still counterfeits the reality of God's power to bring confusion to people. For example, God provides Christians with spiritual gifts such as prophecy and supernatural words of knowledge and wisdom (*1 Corinthians 12*). The Devil provides a counterfeit alternative such as psychics and mediums who pretend to have supernatural information from God or dead people. The Holy Spirit enabled the Apostle Paul and enables Christians to pray the perfect will of God directly to God by praying in tongues. The Devil tries to duplicate this gift in Devil worship ceremonies. People in pagan nations may have a ceremony to try to appease the spirits in their midst by killing a chicken, drinking its blood and dancing around in a demon-induced stupor, supposedly "speaking in tongues." This is not inspired by the Spirit of God, but if people see that on television, they associate a true, precious gift of God with something demonic. Sex is a gift given by God to be enjoyed between a man and a woman who have committed their lives to each other in marriage. Satan takes sex, which is pure and holy, and perverts it by telling people it can be equally enjoyed with a person of the same sex or even a child. Remember, one tactic of the Devil is to take what is God's and pervert it from its original purpose.

POWER SOURCES

God's power is good, positive and uplifting. Satan's power is bad, negative and degrading. Man (mankind – both male and female) is neutral and can choose to submit to either power. The power of choice is a wonderful thing. God gave man the ability to choose. He told His original creation to choose life and obedience. Unfortunately, Adam and Eve chose disobedience which produced death.

God created you as a three-part being. Your spirit is the eternal part of you. Your soul is your mental and emotional component. Your body is the outer, physical part of you. God's desire is that all three parts of your being would be sanctified, or set apart, to Him. God wants you to keep all three parts of your being pure and uncontaminated from the influence of Satan.

Now may the God of peace Himself sanctify you completely; and may your whole spirit, soul, and body be preserved blameless at the coming of our Lord Jesus Christ. (1 Thessalonians 5:23)

Is there such a thing as demon possession? What about demon oppression? Can a Christian be possessed by a demon? These questions come from putting too much emphasis on words like "possession" and "oppression." The original texts of the Bible do not use these words. The Greek word referring to demon control most commonly used in the Bible is "daimonizomai" which describes people as being "demonized." That means a person can be controlled in various degrees by demons. A Christian can learn to be more and more submitted to and controlled by the Holy Spirit. In the same way, a person can learn to be more and more submitted to and controlled by a demon spirit. Demons don't just jump on people and take control of their lives. They start with influencing a person in one area. If you give them control in one small area, they will attempt to take control in another small area. Eventually, a person can allow a demon or demons to control a large part of his life. But it doesn't happen in an instant. Demons control a person one step at a time. I will show you later in this chapter how to prevent demons from gaining access to your life.

People still have a free will, to a certain extent, no matter how much they have submitted to demon control. For example, we find a man described as being "demonized" by "legions" (thousands) of demons, but when Jesus arrived on the scene, the man was still able to go to Jesus for help.

> *And when He stepped out on the land, there met Him a certain man from the city who had demons for a long time. And he wore no clothes, nor did he live in a house but in the tombs. When he saw Jesus, he cried out, fell down before Him, and with a loud voice said, "What have I to do with You, Jesus, Son of the Most High God? I beg You, do not torment me!" For He had commanded the unclean spirit to come out of the man. For it had often seized him, and he was kept under guard, bound with chains and shackles; and he broke the bonds and was driven by the demon into the wilderness. Jesus asked him, saying, "What is your name?" And he said, "Legion," because many demons had entered him. (Luke 8:27-30)*

So what can a demon do to a Christian? God moves into a person's spirit in the Person of the Holy Spirit when that person is born again. Since the Holy Spirit lives in a Christian's spirit, demons cannot "possess" or totally control the spirit of a believer. Your spirit is safe from the enemy if you are a Christian.

"And I will pray the Father, and He will give you another Helper, that He may abide with you forever— "the Spirit of truth, whom the world cannot receive, because it neither sees Him nor knows Him; but you know Him, for He dwells with you and will be in you. (John 14:16-17)

What about demonic influence in the soul (mind and emotions) and the body? Some have thought once you are saved you cannot be touched by demons. That would be a big mistake to think you are immune from demon control because you are a Christian. Paul wrote a letter to all the Christians in Rome and addressed this topic. This letter was written to born again believers.

I beseech you therefore, brethren, by the mercies of God, that you present your bodies a living sacrifice, holy, acceptable to God, which is your reasonable service. And do not be conformed to this world, but be transformed by the renewing of your mind, that you may prove what is that good and acceptable and perfect will of God. (Romans 12:1-2)

Paul is writing to Christians and he says "you" have to make a decision to present your bodies to God. That means a believer with the Holy Spirit living inside can still choose what to do with his body. A Christian can use his body to have sex with a prostitute, take drugs, get drunk or do any number of ungodly things. A Christian can also choose to lift up his hands and worship God with his voice. Notice he also said a Christian will have to renew his mind. A Christian can allow his mind to run wild or choose to align it with God's will. The mind and body have limited power of their own. They can submit to the power of God or the power of demons.

Therefore do not let sin reign in your mortal body, that you should obey it in its lusts. And do not present your members as instruments of unrighteousness to sin, but present yourselves to God as being

*alive from the dead, and your members as instru-
ments of righteousness to God. For sin shall not
have dominion over you, for you are not under law
but under grace. (Romans 6:12-14)*

<u>DEMON INFLUENCE STARTS WITH A THOUGHT</u>. If you want to stay free from demonic control, you must learn to control your thoughts. Have you ever had crazy, immoral thoughts come into your mind? Of course you have. We all have. That does not mean you are demon controlled. You have a choice when a thought contrary to God's will comes into your mind. You can dwell on it and enjoy it or your can reject it and push it aside.

*For though we walk in the flesh, we do not war
according to the flesh. For the weapons of our
warfare are not carnal but mighty in God for pull-
ing down strongholds, <u>casting down</u> arguments and
every high thing that exalts itself against the knowledge of God, <u>bringing every thought into captivity</u>
to the obedience of Christ, (2 Corinthians 10:3-5)*

God said to "cast down" every thought that is contrary to the knowledge and truth of God. I occasionally get sales calls on my home phone. Usually I am polite and tell the person I am not interested in their product or service. They may try to persist, but I tell them I am not interested, thanks for calling, goodbye and then I hang up. Sometimes, though, I am involved in a project or in a hurry to go and I am more abrupt and simply tell the caller, "I am not interested" and immediately hang up the phone. That is the way you have to be when the Devil wants to plant a thought in your head. You don't have to be polite to him. Just tell him, "I cast down that thought, in the name of Jesus!" <u>You have to "hang up" on the Devil</u>. Don't chat with him like Eve did in the Garden of Eden. Just tell him "NO!" and hang up.

I have a friend who was once a drug dealer. He told me he had this thought one time, "I wonder what it would feel like to kill someone?" Where do you think that thought originated? From the Devil!

Thank God my friend never acted on that thought. He is now saved and living for God.

Several years ago America had a series of school shootings. Students decided they would kill other students or teachers who had mistreated them. Do you think these students decided that morning to kill others? No, they didn't. Those actions started with a thought. Satan planted a thought in their heads like this, "Those punks think they are better than you. You don't have to take that. They deserve to die." Those students began to dwell on those thoughts instead of casting them down. Those thoughts grew into a specific plan. They imagined what it would feel like to kill those people who they felt had wronged them. Their anger grew over weeks and months until they developed a plan and put action to their thoughts. But it all started with a thought. If the thought had been cast down immediately, those horrible tragedies could have been avoided.

AREAS OF DEMON INFLUENCE

The Bible many times describes demons by their area of influence. Here are several examples. I have added underlining to the Scriptures to highlight this point.

> *And behold, there was a woman who had a spirit of infirmity eighteen years, and was bent over and could in no way raise herself up. (Luke 13:11)*

> *When Jesus saw that the people came running together, He rebuked the unclean spirit, saying to it, "Deaf and dumb spirit, I command you, come out of him and enter him no more!" (Mark 9:25)*

> *And when He had come out of the boat, immediately there met Him out of the tombs a man with an unclean spirit, (Mark 5:2)*

> *Then one was brought to Him who was demon-possessed, blind and mute; and He healed him, so*

*that the blind and mute man both spoke and saw.
(Matthew 12:22)*

*"The L*ORD *said to him, 'In what way?' So he said,
'I will go out and be a <u>lying spirit</u> in the mouth of
all his prophets'... (1 Kings 22:22)*

*Now the Spirit expressly says that in latter times some
will depart from the faith, giving heed to <u>deceiving
spirits</u> and doctrines of demons, (1 Timothy 4:1)*

*Then one of the crowd answered and said,
"Teacher, I brought You my son, who has a <u>mute
spirit</u>. (Mark 9:17)*

*'Give no regard to mediums and <u>familiar spirits</u>; do
not seek after them, to be defiled by them: I am the
L*ORD *your God. (Leviticus 19:31)*

Most of these are self-explanatory. A blind spirit would be a spirit
that has taken away someone's sight. A mute spirit keeps a person
from talking. A lying spirit motivates a person to lie constantly.
An unclean spirit induces a person to live an unclean lifestyle. For
example, you have probably read in the newspaper sometime about
a Child Protective Services worker finding a mother and her children living in a home infested with insects and rats with rotting
food lying out everywhere and the children covered with filth. Why
would a person live like this? Because an unclean spirit is in control.
Familiar spirits will be discussed in detail later.

*Now the Spirit expressly says that in latter times some
will depart from the faith, giving heed to <u>deceiving
spirits</u> and doctrines of demons, (1 Timothy 4:1)*

I told you earlier that DECEPTION is the Devil's favorite tool.
One definition of "deceive" is "to cause to accept as true or valid
what is false or invalid." An alternate description of the word is,

"imposing a false idea or belief that causes ignorance, bewilderment, or helplessness." A deceiving spirit wants to confuse you into thinking something is good or from God when it is actually bad or from the Devil. If you choose to get involved in activities controlled by Satan and demons, you are opening the door to demonic activity in your life.

I have lived in southern states all my life. Mosquitoes are common in the summer in the south. If I open all the doors and windows in my house and remove the window screens I am going to be swatting mosquitoes all night long. I will constantly be scratching mosquito bites. Wouldn't it be foolish of me to complain to my neighbors, "I don't know why I have so many mosquitoes in my house. They are driving me crazy." My neighbors would probably shake their heads and say, "If you don't want mosquitoes in your house, shut the windows and doors!" Whose fault would it be that I had so many mosquito bites? It would be my fault because I allowed them into my house through my choice of opening the windows and doors. Just because there are mosquitoes in the area doesn't mean they have to be allowed into my house.

The same thing is true of demons. Just because demons are all over the Earth, you don't have to let them into your life. You choose to open the door to your life or keep it shut. You can choose to be involved in occult activities and open the door to demon control in your life or you can choose to refuse to be involved in these activities. Here are some demonic door-openers you should avoid if you want to keep demons out of your life.

Approximately 1/3 of American adults read their horoscope in a typical month. Some of you are probably saying, "Oh, chill out, Randy. I read my horoscope in the paper but it's just for fun. I don't really pay attention to it." Horoscopes pretend to predict your future by the position of the planets in the sky. Think about it. Planets are big rocks. Are you going to take advice from a rock? Why don't you go in your back yard and find some rocks to talk to about which job to take? Do you think what I am saying is ridiculous? It really isn't. If you don't pay attention to your horoscope, then don't read it regularly. The sad news is that approximately 1/3 of <u>Christian adults</u> read their horoscope in a typical month, also! Christians should be looking to God for direction, not the planets. Don't be deceived. Worship the Creator instead of His creation. It's your choice. Open the door to demons or keep it closed.

Have you ever driven by a house with a sign outside that looks like a big hand? A palm reader wants you to come inside so "Madam Watusi" can tell your future by the lines on your hand. She will only look at your palm after you slide some greenbacks into her palm. She may claim to have a "gift from God" to read your palm, but it is another form of deception. You may say, "I only do that for fun. It doesn't mean anything." It means you are choosing to get your guidance from someone other than God. It's your choice. Open the door to demons or keep it closed.

SUPERNATURAL CONTACT

What about séances and mediums? A séance is supposedly an opportunity for living people to talk to dead people through a medium. A medium claims to have an ability to contact the dead and have the dead person speak through them. They do this in several ways. Some have a séance under the cover of darkness or in a dimly lit room. Others have television shows where they do "readings" for people in the studio audience or you can pay them for a private group reading. A "reading" is where the medium claims to be communicating with the dearly departed loved ones of people in the audience or group. This is a dangerous place to be. God never told anyone to speak to dead people. In fact, God actually forbids people to try to do that. You may have been amazed watching these shows and seeing the medium seem to have information that only the dead person would know about. I will explain how this is done shortly. You may be tempted to seek out a medium and have them talk to your deceased relative or friend. It's your choice. Open the door to demons or keep it closed.

How about psychics? Don't these people have a gift from God to be able to help guide you through life? Or maybe you have been told you should get in touch with your "spirit guide" who will give you advice about life. Maybe you have consulted psychics and were astonished to hear them tell you things about your life they would have no way of knowing without supernatural revelation. The truth is some psychics <u>do</u> have supernatural revelation about your life. But they don't get that information from God. I am going to shine the light of truth on psychics, mediums, palm readers, spirit guides and any other kind of supernatural guidance that comes from any source except God and the Holy Spirit.

There are two kinds of psychics. One kind is a total fraud. Their goal is to keep you on the phone line at $3.95/minute for as long as possible. They have a list of common phrases and ailments they use to make you think they have supernatural information about you. For example, the psychic may say something like, "I sense you have had some changes in your life lately." Or maybe they say, "I sense you have had some emotional hurt recently." If you want to believe in them, you will jump on statements like these and allow yourself to be deceived. EVERYONE has had changes in life or emotional hurt at some time.

The other kind of psychic is one who is accessing the supernatural realm for information. However, they are not consulting God. They are consulting demon spirits. This can apply to psychics, mediums, palm readers or anyone else who claims to have information about you that they would have no other way of knowing. They also usually charge a fee for their services. These people are in contact with a "familiar spirit." You will find 16 references to familiar spirits in the Bible. What is a familiar spirit?

We already established that demon spirits were created by God. They were not evil in their original condition. They became corrupted somehow and are now the enemies of God and under the control of Satan. These demon spirits are created beings. They are spirits and do not have the ability to multiply. Demon spirits don't meet another demon spirit, fall in love, get married and have baby demons. You may have thought your neighbor's children might be demons, but they are not! They just need to be disciplined properly! That means the same number of evil spirits exist on Earth today as have always been on Earth. So demons have been around a long time. They become "familiar" with a part of the country, a city, a family, etc., because they have been around them for so long. A person can learn to listen to a familiar spirit without even knowing that is what they are doing.

The philosophy of reincarnation is a good example of how a familiar spirit can deceive or "cause to accept as true or valid what is false or invalid." Reincarnation is the belief that when a person dies, he is reborn as a different person and lives another life. The Hindu and Scientology cults are examples of some that advocate this belief. This false doctrine describes a continuing living and dying and coming back again. Your new life is supposedly based on how well you did in your previous life. If you did a good job, your new life will be better than the previous one. If you made a lot of mistakes, your next life will be worse than the previous one while you work out your "karma." The idea is you keep learning lessons and getting a new opportunity to "get it right" with each new life. The truth of the matter is you only get one chance at life and death. None of us live a perfect life. We all make mistakes. That is why we need Jesus. Jesus made it possible for our mistakes to be forgiven and to help us recover when we mess up.

> *And as it is appointed for men to die once, but after this the judgment, (Hebrews 9:27)*

I remember reading a book about reincarnation when I was in my teens. The book described a young girl who felt that she had lived a previous life. She was hypnotized and allowed the hypnotist to do an "age regression" with her. The age regression supposedly took this girl back in time through her hidden memories. The hypnotist purportedly took her far enough back in time to where she remembered her "previous life." The young lady described a scene in another country where she thought she grew up in her previous life. She described in great detail the house she lived in, a path to a well the family used, who her neighbors were and many other things about the area. After recording all her observations, the authors of the book took a trip to the country this girl described as being the scene of a previous life before she was reincarnated into the present one she was living. Amazingly, they found her descriptions to be accurate. Everything was just as she described. Research showed the people who were her neighbors really did live nearby a long time ago. I was astonished! I thought this proved reincarnation to be a valid experience. But I did not know about familiar spirits. I was a young teenage boy, and I was deceived.

This is what happened. Demon spirits who had existed in that area for thousands of years became "familiar" with that part of that country. They knew about that house and the well and the family who lived next door. This young lady opened her mind up to listen to a familiar spirit. She probably didn't choose to do it. She may not have known anything about the spirit world where demons operate. Hypnotism is a process where you essentially put your mind in neutral. You become very susceptible to suggestions from the hypnotist. She also became susceptible to input from a supernatural demon spirit. This familiar spirit began to describe a scene that was well-known to him since he lived there for a long time. It would be as if you put the phone to your ear and listened to me describe my house and neighborhood. You could repeat all that information to someone and they would think you must have visited my house to be able to describe it in such detail. The truth would be you only listened to someone very familiar with the house describe it. This young girl did not live a previous life in another country. She only listened to a familiar spirit describe something with which he was familiar.

Psychics, palm readers, mediums and channelers all get their information the same way. They are contacting familiar spirits. For example, a person may consult one of these types and hear them say something like, "You just broke up with your boyfriend, Bob, didn't you?" You are amazed because what she said is true! How did she know about that? She knew because there are familiar spirits who know about you and your life and will be happy to "tell on you" to someone willing to listen to them. A medium who claims to be able to talk to someone who is dead is the same way. They may relate intimate details about the deceased person or their family members because they are listening to a familiar spirit who can give them that information.

Here is why you need to know about these deceptions. All these deceiving spirits are out to accomplish the same thing. THEY WANT TO DIRECT YOUR ATTENTION AWAY FROM GOD

TO SOMETHING ELSE. This is how the deception works. If you consult a psychic, she may be able to tell you something about your past. If you begin to put your trust in this person because she supernaturally knew something about your past, the Devil can begin to control your future. If you trust this person as a source of supernatural guidance, the Devil can take you down a path he has designed for you by pretending to know your future. The familiar spirit may tell you to divorce your spouse or quit your job or end a friendship with a godly person. Demons can't tell you what will happen in your future like God can. But if they can influence you to bypass God for your guidance, they can keep you from fulfilling God's destiny for you.

The Holy Spirit will promote and glorify Jesus. People controlled by familiar spirits usually promote and glorify themselves. The Holy Spirit will give you information to help you grow closer to God and accomplish good in your life. Familiar spirits seek to control and manipulate and make you dependent on people instead of God. Familiar spirits help promote spiritual laziness. The Devil's deception through familiar spirits attempts to influence you to bypass spending time reading the Bible, going to church, praying and talking to other Christians about God. Demons try to convince you to take a short cut by calling a psychic or going to a palm reader or medium to get guidance.

God's guidance can come from several sources. His word, the Bible, is the most important source to access. When you know the Bible, you can more easily recognize the counterfeit guidance that comes from Satan. The Holy Spirit will give you direction and understanding in your spirit. His direction will never contradict what you find written in the Bible. Godly people, such as pastors, teachers and friends, can bring you direction also. Notice that none of these sources require a fee like the Devil's deceptions.

DEMON ASSIGNMENTS

Demon spirits can be assigned to countries, states, cities and families. Familiar spirits can continue to influence families through generations if left unchecked. A Christian must recognize demons at work and stop their activity in that family. Daniel was an Old

Testament prophet who went on a three-week time of fasting and prayer to know and understand God's plans for his people. At the conclusion of his fast, he received a vision from God about the future and a visit from an angel to help him understand the vision. The angel made an interesting statement that confirms the fact that demons can be assigned to regions of the world.

> *Then he said, "Don't be afraid, Daniel. Since the first day you began to pray for understanding and to humble yourself before your God, your request has been heard in Heaven. I have come in answer to your prayer. But for twenty-one days <u>the spirit prince of the kingdom of Persia blocked my way</u>. Then Michael, one of the archangels, came to help me, and I left him there with the spirit prince of the kingdom of Persia. (Daniel 10:12-13)(NLT)*

The angel said after he was dispatched to Daniel he encountered great resistance coming through Persia. A demon spirit (assigned by Satan to control that country) kept God's angel from passing through. One of God's most powerful angels, Michael, had to go to Persia to help fight off Satan's demon to allow the angel to pass through and reach Daniel. Satan most likely has demon spirits assigned to certain countries and cities still today. Surely Satan has demons of communism and atheism assigned to China to keep the gospel out. Demons of homosexuality are assigned to San Francisco. Demons of lust and gambling are assigned to Las Vegas (what demons do in Vegas, stays in Vegas!). Demons of perversion are assigned to New Orleans. This does not mean Christians can't exist and prosper in those places. When you know your authority and how to use it, you can overcome the enemy. It means that Satan has a stronghold of control in that region to influence people for evil. This happens because demons have established control in that place over a long period of time.

The same is true of families. When the same pattern of behavior and problems continues to manifest in generation after generation of a family, many times a familiar spirit has gained control and must be removed. For example, if Great-Grandpa regularly cheated on his wife and Grandpa regularly cheated on his wife and Dad regularly cheated on his wife, and the son regularly cheats on his wife, there is likely a demon spirit who has been unknowingly welcomed into that family for generations. The same can be said for families with generations of alcoholism, drug addiction, homosexuality, multiple divorces etc. <u>Demon spirits are real and must be dealt with instead of allowing them to remain in control.</u> I will begin to describe how to deal with demons later in this chapter.

DOCTRINES OF DEMONS

Now the Spirit expressly says that in latter times some will depart from the faith, giving heed to deceiving spirits and <u>doctrines of demons</u>, (1 Timothy 4:1)

A "doctrine" is a teaching or particular belief system. You can believe doctrines from God or you can believe doctrines of demons. Doctrines of demons usually lead you to a works-based relationship with God instead of one based on God's grace. The Mormon doctrine is an example of a "doctrine of demons." The founder of Mormonism was a man named Joseph Smith. He claims to have had a visitation from an angel who brought him additional revelation about Jesus. Maybe you know some Mormons and think they are wonderful Christian people. They may be good people, but their doctrine came from a demon and not from God. Their doctrine teaches that a Christian can work his way up to being a god over a planet. They believe the God who rules our planet was once a man who worked his way up to being God. Salvation in their view is based on works – doing enough good things to earn God's favor.

People can be <u>sincere</u> in their beliefs, but can be <u>sincerely wrong</u> in their beliefs. Jehovah's Witnesses and Mormons go door-to-door attempting to persuade people to join their religious groups. These people are good people. They don't wake up in the morning and say, "I wonder how many people we can deceive today?" They think they are right in their beliefs. They have been deceived by doctrines of demons that take them away from the simplicity of the gospel message. God's doctrine points people to Jesus as the only answer to their sin problem. Paul described the Jewish people of his day as sincere people with a passion for what they believed. However, what they believed was wrong. They tried to earn their right standing with God instead of receiving God's grace through Jesus Christ.

> *Brethren, my heart's desire and prayer to God for Israel is that they may be saved. For I bear them witness that <u>they have a zeal for God, but not according to knowledge</u>. For they <u>being ignorant</u> of God's righteousness, and seeking to establish their own righteousness, have not submitted to the righteousness of God. For Christ is the end of the law for righteousness to everyone who believes. (Romans 10:1-4)*

DEALING WITH DEMONS

Jesus' ministry activities involved four main areas – preaching, teaching, healing and casting out demons.

> *And Jesus went about all Galilee, teaching in their synagogues, preaching the gospel of the kingdom, and healing all kinds of sickness and all kinds of disease among the people. Then His fame went throughout all Syria; and they brought to Him all sick people who were afflicted with various diseases and torments, and those who were demon-possessed, epileptics, and paralytics; and He healed them. (Matthew 4:23-24)*

Jesus said those who believe on him should do the same things He did while He was on the Earth and teach others to do the same things He did.

> *"Most assuredly, I say to you, he who believes in Me, the works that I do he will do also; and greater*

works than these he will do, because I go to My
Father. (John 14:12)

"Go therefore and make disciples of all the nations,
baptizing them in the name of the Father and of
the Son and of the Holy Spirit, "teaching them to
observe all things that I have commanded you; and
lo, I am with you always, even to the end of the age."
Amen. (Matthew 28:19-20)

One of the things Jesus did while on the Earth was cast out
demons. If we are to follow His command to do what He did and
teach others to do what He did, we are going to have to cast out
demons. Jesus said one of the signs of a believer would be that he
would cast out demons.

"And these signs will follow those who believe: In
My name they will cast out demons... (Mark 16:17)

You may not like talking about demons. This subject probably
doesn't come up much when you are at your job. If you tell your
co-workers at lunch that you are studying about casting out demons,
they may quickly excuse themselves and avoid you at all costs! But
Jesus said <u>believers</u> should understand about demons so we can cast
them out. He did not say only full-time, ordained members of the
clergy would cast demons out. He said <u>those who believe</u> would
cast out demons. Since Jesus cast out demons with the authority of
a man without sin, we should look at Jesus to see how to do it. It
really is very simple. <u>Jesus cast out demons by speaking to them and</u>
<u>commanding them to leave</u>.

Now there was a man in their synagogue with
an unclean spirit. And he cried out, saying, "Let
us alone! What have we to do with You, Jesus of
Nazareth? Did You come to destroy us? I know
who You are—the Holy One of God!" But Jesus
rebuked him, saying, "Be quiet, and come out of

him!" And when the unclean spirit had convulsed him and cried out with a loud voice, he came out of him. Then they were all amazed, so that they questioned among themselves, saying, "What is this? What new doctrine is this? For with authority He commands even the unclean spirits, and they obey Him." (Mark 1:23-27)

You can cast out demons the same way by speaking to them and telling them to leave. People have invented all kinds of ways to deal with demons, but the best method is to follow Jesus' example and command them to leave. There is nothing in the Bible about having to read a certain prayer, use certain phrases or use some sort of religious apparatus or icon to have authority over demons. Your authority comes from Jesus and the victory He gave you over sin. You speak to demons in the name of Jesus with the authority He gave you. You can command demons to leave your house, a person's body, your marriage relationship, your work location or any other place they set up shop and try to cause problems. Demons are most effective and comfortable when they can control and influence individuals. However, they can also be assigned to disrupt gatherings of people such as a work environment, a family or even a church. Satan takes great pleasure if he can infiltrate a local church and cause division to the point of a church split or cause a pastor to be fired or leave because he is tired of the turmoil.

Once you were dead, doomed forever because of your many sins. You used to live just like the rest of the world, full of sin, obeying Satan, the mighty prince of the power of the air. He is the spirit at work in the hearts of those who refuse to obey God. (Ephesians 2:1-2)(NLT)

The Greek word in this Scripture translated "air" as in "prince of the power of the air," refers to the atmosphere above the Earth. That is Satan's primary domain. He and his demons have the freedom to roam and operate on the Earth, in our atmosphere. They don't have authority over a Christian, but they do have a right to be on the Earth. Here is an example of how Paul dealt with a demon spirit. A fortune-teller kept following Paul and his team around telling people they were sent by God. She got that right, but would you want a demonized fortune-teller advertising your ministry? Paul did not want her to gain any credibility by attaching herself to them. Eventually, he got irritated when he realized she was demon-controlled and listening to familiar spirits for a fee.

> *One day as we were going down to the place of prayer, we met a demon-possessed slave girl. She was a fortune-teller who earned a lot of money for her masters. She followed along behind us shouting, "These men are servants of the Most High God, and they have come to tell you how to be saved."*
>
> *This went on day after day until Paul got so exasperated that he turned and spoke to the demon within her. "I command you in the name of Jesus Christ to come out of her," he said. And instantly it left her. (Acts 16:16-18)(NLT)*

Paul finally had enough of this woman and her demon. Notice how he dealt with her. He did the same thing Jesus did to get rid of a demon. He spoke to the spirit in the name of Jesus and told him to leave. The spirit obeyed Paul because of Paul's authority. He did not have to call for someone with a special "deliverance ministry." He didn't read a special prayer. He just commanded him to leave. The Devil is not very creative. He continues to try the same tricks today. If an incident like this happened today it would sound something like this:

> *As I turned on the television, a certain psychic hotline girl, possessed with a familiar spirit who brought her employers much profit by enticing people to talk to her for $3.95/minute, claimed she had a gift from God to tell my fortune.*

GIFTS OF THE SPIRIT

How do you know if you are dealing with a demon who must be cast out or a person who is just a jerk? One way is if God supernaturally reveals the truth to you through a gift of the Holy Spirit. The Bible describes some of these gifts in *1 Corinthians 12:7-11*. One is called a "Word of Knowledge" which is a supernatural revelation from the Holy Spirit about a fact, past or present. This is a gift which is counterfeited by demons when familiar spirits reveal something about your past or present. There can be no counterfeit unless there is the original and real. The Holy Spirit can reveal to you that a person is controlled by a demon. Another gift of the Holy Spirit is called "Discerning of Spirits" which is a supernatural revealing of the spirit realm where God allows a person to see into this realm and identify demons or even angels. These are gifts that operate as the Holy Spirit wills. You cannot turn them on and off even if you have seen these gifts work in your life previously.

Another way is to recognize the activity of the person to see if it matches the way demons act. I was preaching in North Carolina one time when I encountered a person controlled by a demon. I finished my sermon and gave a general altar call for people to come forward for prayer. A petite young woman walked up to me and I said to her, "What can I pray with you about?" She responded by saying, "I cut myself." I said, "What do you mean, you cut yourself?" She said again, "I cut myself." The Holy Spirit immediately brought a Scripture to my mind that described an encounter Jesus had with a demonized man.

Then they came to the other side of the sea, to the country of the Gadarenes. And when He had come out of the boat, immediately there met Him out of the tombs a man with an <u>unclean spirit</u>, who had his dwelling among the tombs; and no one could bind him, not even with chains, because he had often been bound with shackles and chains. And the chains had been pulled apart by him, and the shackles broken in pieces; neither could anyone

tame him. And always, night and day, he was in the
mountains and in the tombs, crying out and <u>cutting</u>
<u>himself</u> with stones. (Mark 5:1-5)

I realized this lady was controlled by a demon that motivated her to cut herself. I found out later she was part of a group of ladies living in a shelter for abused women. The physical abuse she had endured was most likely from the hand of a demon-controlled man. This abuse probably opened the door for a demon to control this woman and tell her she was no good and needed to be punished for being so bad. Cutting her own body was a way to punish herself.

I looked into the woman's eyes and spoke directly to the demon. I said, "In the name of Jesus, I command you to leave this woman." When the woman first approached me, she was shy and very quiet. However, her demeanor changed quickly once I spoke to the demon. Her body stiffened and her eyes filled with hate as she stared at me. <u>She</u> didn't hate me, but the demon did. The demon spoke through her to reply to me and say, "I don't have to leave. She wants me here." Remember, the Devil and demons are liars. She did not really want to be controlled by a demon. That is why she came forward for prayer. She wanted to be set free. Just like the man we read about in the Scripture above. Even though he had been almost totally controlled by demons, he came to Jesus because he wanted to be free. I knew not to argue or negotiate with demons. I said, "In the name of Jesus, I command you to leave. You have no right to stay." The demon spoke back and said, "We'll be here all night because I am not leaving." I said, "No, we will not be here all night because you have to obey me. In the name of Jesus, I command you to come out of her."

Sometimes demons can be stubborn. They will test you to see if you really believe what you are saying. It took me approximately 15 minutes to get that demon to leave. He kept saying things like, "You can't make me leave." But I was persistent and would not give up. I continued to command that demon to leave and I always used the name of Jesus. Finally, the demon left. The young lady's body relaxed and she began to cry. I explained to her how to be saved and led her in a prayer to receive Jesus as her Savior. Her face lit up with the joy of the Lord as we all celebrated her new freedom from the bondage of the enemy. She left that church with a peace and freedom she had never known.

DEMONS WANT TO RETURN

Remember that demons control a person over a period of time. People learn to relinquish control a little bit at a time. When a person does not understand what is happening, a demon or demons can become very much a part of a person's life without them even knowing what is happening. As strange as it may seem, a person who has been controlled by demons for a long time thinks their control is "normal." Because they think it is normal, they are susceptible to demons coming back even after they have been cast out. Demons find their greatest expression through a human being. When they are cast out, they will want to come back. Jesus explained it like this:

> *"When an unclean spirit goes out of a man, he goes through dry places, seeking rest, and finds none. "Then he says, 'I will return to my house from which I came.' And when he comes, he finds it empty, swept, and put in order. "Then he goes and takes with him seven other spirits more wicked than himself, and they enter and dwell there; and the last state of that man is worse than the first. So shall it also be with this wicked generation."* *(Matthew 12:43-45)*

Notice the spirit says he will go back to *"my house."* He can make a home in a person if that person has learned to submit to him. He will try to return and bring more of his nasty buddies with him if his former *"house"* is *"empty."* After you free people from demonic control, make sure they are born again so demons will have no access to that person's spirit. Then you must help them receive the baptism of the Holy Spirit so they will have that extra power to resist sin and the Devil. Next, you need to help them learn to feed their mind and spirit a steady diet of the Word of God to build up their faith and bring revelation about their authority to resist the Devil. They also need to find a good church to attend regularly and develop a new set of friends to be around. Help them to avoid the former hangouts, activities and people who took them into the Devil's territory. For example, if a person is delivered from a demon of pornography, he may need to terminate his internet service for awhile so he won't be tempted to return. If a person is delivered from homosexuality, he doesn't need to immediately be going into gay bars to try to convert his former friends. An alcoholic needs new people to socialize with who don't spend time where alcohol is served. Don't make it easy for a demon to return to a place he was once welcomed.

NO FEAR

Learning about demons should not make you afraid of them. Remember, Satan and his demons have been disarmed. When you are free from sin, they have no control over you unless you allow it. With Jesus in you, the Devil is not someone to fear.

> *You are of God, little children, and have overcome them, because He who is in you is greater than he who is in the world. (1 John 4:4)*

CHASING DEMONS

Jesus granted temporary authority over demons to a group of 70 followers while He was still on the Earth. They were amazed at their ability to control demons. Using their authority was the main topic of conversation when they got back together. In the same way, reading a book like this may get you all stirred up to think the most important thing you can do is cast out demons. A danger of getting filled up with all this wonderful revelation is you can become unbalanced in your approach to life. Look what Jesus said to get their focus back where it belonged.

> *After these things the Lord appointed seventy others also, and sent them two by two before His face into*

every city and place where He Himself was about to go. (Luke 10:1)

Then the seventy returned with joy, saying, "Lord, even the demons are subject to us in Your name." And He said to them, "I saw Satan fall like lightning from Heaven. "Behold, I give you the authority to trample on serpents and scorpions, and over all the power of the enemy, and nothing shall by any means hurt you. "Nevertheless do not rejoice in this, that the spirits are subject to you, but rather rejoice because your names are written in Heaven." (Luke 10:17-20)

Jesus said the source of your joy should be that your name is written in Heaven more than that you can cast out demons. Telling people about the salvation Jesus offers is a higher priority than casting out demons. When people are born again, they gain the freedom from sin that gives them authority over demons. You won't have to deal with demons every day. As you go about your business, when you encounter demon spirits controlling or influencing a person or group, cast them out. But don't spend all day every day looking for demons to fight just because you can.

---

[1] The Barna Group Website, 2005, Barna By Topic, Beliefs: Trinity, Satan, www. barna.org, Ventura, CA

CHAPTER 9

THE NAME OF JESUS

Access control is a major industry in today's world. Keys used to be the primary way to control access, but that is no longer the case. Now we have cards with magnetic stripes, cards that emit radio signals, fingerprint readers and even equipment that can scan your retina to make sure you have permission to open a door. All those methods are to ensure only certain people can gain access to critical data, equipment or individuals.

What about access to God? What kind of control system allows a person to receive all God has to offer? Some people believe all religions are essentially the same. Many contend that all you have to do is believe in a "higher power" and your access to God is insured. But what does Jesus say about that?

> *"Let not your heart be troubled; you believe in God, believe also in Me. "In My Father's house are many mansions; if it were not so, I would have told you. I go to prepare a place for you. "And if I go and prepare a place for you, I will come again and receive you to Myself; that where I am, there you may be also. "And where I go you know, and the way you know." Thomas said to Him, "Lord, we do not know where You are going, and how can we know the way?" Jesus said to him, "I am the way,*

> *the truth, and the life. No one comes to the Father*
> *except through Me. (John 14:1-6)*

I read a statistic that revealed 56% of non-Christian Americans believe it doesn't matter what faith you follow because they all teach the same lessons.1 Jesus made the truth very clear in the statement referenced above. Jesus did not say He was "one of many ways to God." He said "no one" comes to the Father any other way except through Him. He left no room for negotiation. "No one" means <u>no one</u>! Jesus always told the truth. People are gambling their eternity away by entertaining thoughts that "any religion will do as long as you believe something."

The religious leaders arrested Peter and John one day because they continued to preach about Jesus even though they had been told to stop. When Peter spoke in defense of his actions, he explained the importance of preaching Jesus.

> *"Nor is there salvation in any other, for there is*
> *no other name under heaven given among men by*
> *which we must be saved." (Acts 4:12)*

There is NO OTHER NAME. It's plain and simple. Peter told them the truth, just as he heard it from Jesus. If you don't trust Jesus, you can't be saved. Some of you may be thinking, "Doesn't everybody know that already?" The answer is, "No!" Approximately 40% of the adult public in America is born again.2 The sad part is this statistic has remained nearly the same for 25 years. How can this be in America? We have an abundance of churches, Christian radio, Christian television, Christian bookstores, Christian websites, Bible schools and seminaries. Here is another shocking statistic: 43% of people who attend church are not born again!3 Why is that true? The only answer I have is that not enough pastors are preaching the truth to their congregations. Perhaps too many pastors preach a "feel-good" message to appeal to the most people possible. Sadly, many of those people will die in their sins and spend eternity in hell because nobody told them the truth! The truth is it takes much more than positive thinking and a mental agreement that Jesus loves us, died on a cross and rose again. It takes a personal decision to trust in Jesus alone for your eternal salvation.

I imagine many of those 43% of people who attend church without being saved think they are Christians because they go to church. However, sitting in church won't make you a Christian any more than living in your garage will make you a car! It takes the cleansing power of Jesus to clean us up from our sins, set us apart to God and justify us in God's sight.

> *Do you not know that the unrighteous will not inherit the kingdom of God? Do not be deceived. Neither fornicators, nor idolaters, nor adulterers, nor homosexuals, nor sodomites, nor thieves, nor covetous, nor drunkards, nor revilers, nor extortioners will inherit the kingdom of God. And such were some of you. But you were <u>washed</u>, but you were <u>sanctified</u>, but you were <u>justified in the name of the Lord Jesus</u> and by the Spirit of our God. (1 Corinthians 6:9-11)*

It is unfortunate, but 54% of Americans believe they can earn a place in Heaven either by "being good" or by "doing enough good things for other people during their life."[4] In other words, <u>over half of Americans see their eternity based on a giant scale of justice</u>. They think when they die, all their sins will be placed on one side of the scale and all their good deeds on the other side. They believe if they have just one more good deed than bad deed (sin), the scales will tip in their favor and they will make it into Heaven. That is why it is vitally important that pastors tell people a complete trust in and commitment to Jesus is necessary to be in right standing with God. If no opportunity is given in a service to make that commitment, it appears to be unimportant. Too many churchgoers think they are on their way to Heaven because they drove the youth group to camp one summer; they help take up the offering every six weeks; they sing in the choir; they teach Sunday school; or some other such "church activity" which will "earn" them favor in God's eyes when He decides who gets into Heaven.

Authority From God

ACCESS TO THE THRONE

Jesus explained His soon-coming departure to His disciples. He knew they would react with great sorrow and tears at his death. But He gave them an analogy to help them work through their grief when it happened. He said it would be like a woman who gives birth to a child. The labor can be difficult and stressful, but when she holds her newborn in her arms, all the pain is forgotten. She is thrilled to be looking into the eyes of her baby. All she can think about now is the future she and her child have together.

Jesus told His disciples they would cry and mourn when He died. But His death would not be the end. He explained they will see Him again after the resurrection and have a joy that cannot be taken away. Then Jesus told them how His resurrection would enable them to have access directly to God.

"A little while, and you will not see Me; and again a little while, and you will see Me, because I go to the Father." Then some of His disciples said among themselves, "What is this that He says to us, 'A little while, and you will not see Me; and again a little while, and you will see Me'; and, 'because I go to the Father'?" They said therefore, "What is this that He says, 'A little while'? We do not know what He is saying." Now Jesus knew that they desired to ask Him, and He said to them, "Are you inquiring among yourselves about what I said, 'A little while, and you will not see Me; and again a little while, and you will see Me'? "Most assuredly, I say to you that you will weep and lament, but the world will rejoice; and you will be sorrowful, but your sorrow will be turned into joy. "A woman, when she is in labor, has sorrow because her hour has come; but as soon as she has given birth to the child, she no longer remembers the anguish, for joy that a human being has been born into the world. "Therefore you now have sorrow; but I will see you again and your

heart will rejoice, and your joy no one will take from you. "And in that day you will ask Me nothing. Most assuredly, I say to you, <u>whatever you ask the Father in My name</u> He will give you. "Until now you have asked nothing in My name. Ask, and you will receive, that your joy may be full. "These things I have spoken to you in figurative language; but the time is coming when I will no longer speak to you in figurative language, but I will tell you plainly about the Father. "In that day you will <u>ask in My name</u>, and I do not say to you that I shall pray the Father for you; "for the Father Himself loves you, because you have loved Me, and have believed that I came forth from God. "I came forth from the Father and have come into the world. Again, I leave the world and go to the Father." (John 16:16-28)

Jesus did not do away with the Old Covenant office of the High Priest. Jesus became the <u>final</u> High Priest and His name gives us the authority to talk to God directly. God will hear your prayers and respond with <u>mercy</u> and <u>grace</u>. What a wonderful truth! You should be glad God doesn't respond with justice. Believe me; you don't want to always get what you deserve. "Mercy" means God **doesn't** give you what you have earned. We have all sinned and deserve to be punished. You should be glad you don't get what you deserve. "Grace" means God **gives** you something you have not earned. Have you lived a perfectly holy life? Of course you haven't. But God wants to give you His blessings, even though you have not earned them. So when you come to God with a need, He will respond with MERCY and GRACE.

That is why we have a great High Priest who has gone to heaven, Jesus the Son of God. Let us cling to him and never stop trusting him. This High Priest of ours understands our weaknesses, for he faced all of the same temptations we do, yet he did not sin. So let us come boldly to the throne of our gracious

God. There we will receive his <u>mercy</u>, and we will find <u>grace</u> to help us when we need it. (Hebrews 4:14-16)(NLT)

Jesus understands the reality of temptation. He was tempted throughout His life on Earth. Yet He never gave in to sin. Some would say it was impossible for Jesus to sin. If that were true, how could His temptations have been real? If He did not have the capability of giving in to sin, the temptations would not have been valid. That is why you can talk to Jesus about your struggles. He faced struggles, also. He knows what you are going through. He knows how to resist evil.

Have you ever tried to get through to someone the world deems "important?" If you are calling on the phone you may get trapped in a voice mail nightmare – "If you speak English, press 1; If you speak Spanish, press 2 – If you have red hair, press 3; If you have blond hair, press 4 – If you know your account number, press 5; If you are too stupid to find your account number, press 6 – If you need more information, go to our website at www.abcdefg.com – If you don't have access to the internet, hang up and get a life – If you thought you were going to talk to a real person, press any button you want because that's not going to happen – If you would like to return to the main menu and waste some more time, press 0." Sometimes it seems impossible to get the "important" person on the phone!

Isn't God the most "important person" in all of eternity? And, because of Jesus, **you** can have the authority to enter **His throne room** and talk to Him any time you want! You will never have an angel intercept your prayer and tell you, "God is away from His desk right now. May I assist you in some way?" You won't get a message saying, "Our office hours are 9:00 a.m. to 5:00 p.m. Central Standard Time." You won't get a busy signal or enter into a voice mail nightmare. Jesus gives you **unlimited access to God**, 24/7!

HEALING IN JESUS' NAME

Jesus delegated to believers the authority to use His name. It is much like the power of attorney. My wife and I once purchased a house while the owners were out of the country. They signed a legal document giving a real estate agent the power of attorney. The real estate agent could sign the necessary documents as if she were the owner because the owners had delegated that authority to her. Believers can now minister healing to others in the same way Jesus did because we have the use of His name. Jesus wants believers to do the same thing He would do if He were still physically living on the Earth. When Jesus encountered sick people, He healed them. When He encountered people controlled by demons, He cast the demons out. He wants believers, as His body on the Earth, to do the same.

> *"And these signs will follow those who believe: In My name they will cast out demons; they will speak with new tongues; "they will take up serpents; and if they drink anything deadly, it will by no means hurt them; they will lay hands on the sick, and they will recover." (Mark 16:17-18)*

Jesus said these signs would follow believers. Does He mean simply those who believe in Him as Savior or could He mean something else? When the New Testament Scriptures were translated from Greek into English, the translators had to decide where the punctuation marks belonged. In the Scripture above, the colon between "believe" and "In" was added by the translators. It is not in the original text. Perhaps the colon doesn't belong there. Maybe it would be better located after the phrase "In My name." Read it out loud both ways and see if it makes a difference.

And these signs will follow those who believe – Stop – In My name they will …

or

And these signs will follow those who believe in My name – Stop – They will…

I am not trying to change the Scriptures. Either way portrays a powerful truth. But it seems to me that believing in the authority and power of the name of Jesus is a critical component of doing what Jesus said to do on His behalf. There is another place in the Bible where believing in Jesus' name is mentioned concerning healing.

> *Is anyone among you sick? Let him call for the elders of the church, and let them pray over him, anointing him with oil in the name of the Lord. And the prayer of faith will save the sick, and the Lord will raise him up. And if he has committed sins, he will be forgiven. (James 5:14-15)*

James describes another method of receiving healing from Jesus. He said to call for spiritually mature people (elders) in the church. This is a way to join people's faith together to accomplish more than is possible with only the faith of one. Joining your faith together for greater results is like the method you use to move a piano. If one person tries to lift and move a piano, the piano isn't going anywhere. But if several people surround the piano and lift all at once, the group can easily handle the weight because of the combination of all their strength. Gathering the elders together is a way of combining the mature faith of a group of people to accomplish more than could be done with only one person believing.

James also said to anoint the person with oil. He gives no special instructions on the type of oil to use. There are no special properties in the oil that produce healing. The oil is symbolic of the Holy Spirit. The oil is applied as a point of contact and a reminder that the power of the Holy Spirit is at work to bring healing to the person receiving prayer. A point of contact is a point in time when a person begins to believe and release the power of faith. All the elders and the person receiving prayer can activate their faith at the same time when the oil is applied.

The next thing James said was to pray in the name of the Lord. What is the name of the Lord? His name is Jesus. So James said for the elders to pray in Jesus' name. Then James said the "prayer of faith" will "save" the sick. The Greek word translated "save" is "sozo," which is an all-inclusive word which means "save, make whole, heal, preserve, or rescue." He said the prayer of faith will "heal and make whole" the sick person. A prayer of faith requires that people "believe" what they are praying. A prayer of faith in the name of the Lord means the people praying must believe in the delegated authority of the name of Jesus. This is the same point I believe Jesus was making when He delegated His authority in *Mark 16*. Remember, He told His followers they could activate His healing power by believing in the delegated authority and power of His name.

When someone is sick, you have authority to use the name of Jesus to bring healing to a sick person. Perhaps when you pray, they will receive an instantaneous healing. Maybe you are their only hope. Maybe if you don't pray for them they will never get well. But what if you pray and they don't get well? I have prayed for people who got healed and I have prayed for people who did not get well. Why is that? We will never have all the answers as to why someone isn't healed. Some things will remain a secret unless God chooses to reveal them to us.

> *"The secret things belong to the LORD our God, but those things which are revealed belong to us and to our children forever, that we may do all the words of this law. (Deuteronomy 29:29)*

If you pray for a sick person in the name of Jesus and you believe for their healing with everything within you, you can sleep at night knowing you did all you knew to do. Our command is to lay hands on the sick and pray in the name of Jesus. God's part is to raise them up and bring healing. If you don't do your part, you limit God in doing His part. Don't worry about what may NOT happen. Believe for the best. I expect everyone I pray for to be healed. And if they don't receive their healing, I rest in the fact I did all I was capable of doing. The unanswered questions I leave with God.

AUTHORITY OVER SATAN

The name of Jesus gives us authority over Satan and his demons. Jesus' name is above every name of Satan, demons, sickness, etc. And now we can use His name and walk in His authority.

Therefore God also has highly exalted Him and given Him the name which is above every name, that at the name of Jesus every knee should bow, of those in heaven, and of those on earth, and of those under the earth, and that every tongue should confess that Jesus Christ is Lord, to the glory of God the Father. (Philippians 2:9-11)

The name of Jesus isn't a "magic word" like "abracadabra." Just saying His name means nothing unless you believe in the authority and power of that name. In fact, if you try to use His name carelessly, it will be like trying to capture a criminal with an unloaded gun. Once the criminal knows your weapon is useless, he will attack you and make you wish you hadn't attempted to bother him. Look at what happened to a group of people who thought they could just say the name of Jesus and get the same results as those who were saved and "believed" in the name.

A team of Jews who were traveling from town to town casting out evil spirits tried to use the name of the Lord Jesus. The incantation they used was this: "I command you by Jesus, whom Paul preaches, to come out!" Seven sons of Sceva, a leading priest, were doing this. But when they tried it on a man possessed by an evil spirit, the spirit replied, "I know Jesus, and I know Paul. But who are you?" And he leaped on them and attacked them with such violence that they fled from the house, naked and badly injured. The story of what happened spread quickly all through Ephesus, to Jews and Greeks alike. A solemn fear descended on the city, and the name of the Lord Jesus was greatly honored. (Acts 19:13-17)(NLT)

Paul used the name of Jesus to deal with a demonized woman who was harassing his ministry team.

... But Paul, greatly annoyed, turned and said to the spirit, "I command you in the name of Jesus Christ to come out of her." And he came out that very hour. (Acts 16:18)

The name of Jesus is a powerful weapon. It is only valuable, however, for those who are born again and believe in the authority and power resident in the name of Jesus.

---

[1] The Barna Group Website, Barna By Topic, Beliefs: Born Again Christians, 2000, www.barna.org, Ventura, CA

[2] The Barna Group Website, Barna By Topic, Beliefs: Born Again Christians, 2005, www.barna.org, Ventura, CA

[3] The State of the Church: 2005, George Barna and The Barna Group, Ventura, CA, Page 7

[4] The State of the Church: 2005, George Barna and The Barna Group, Ventura, CA, Page 37

CHAPTER 10

TWO KINGDOMS

You live in one of two kingdoms. In the eternal realm of the spirit, you only have two choices. The spirit realm is just as real as the physical realm you contact with your senses. The spiritual kingdom in which you live is either ruled by Jesus or Satan. Every one of us at one time lived in the kingdom of darkness which is ruled by the Devil. Before a person is saved, he is subject to Satan because of sin. Once your sin is removed by trusting in the blood of Jesus, you are transferred into the kingdom where Jesus rules. Paul made this very clear when he wrote a letter to the Christians in the city of Colosse. His letter included this prayer:

> *So we have continued praying for you ever since we first heard about you. We ask God to give you a complete understanding of what he wants to do in your lives, and we ask him to make you wise with spiritual wisdom. Then the way you live will always honor and please the Lord, and you will continually do good, kind things for others. All the while, you will learn to know God better and better. We also pray that you will be strengthened with his glorious power so that you will have all the patience and endurance you need. May you be filled with joy, always thanking the Father, who has enabled you*

to share the inheritance that belongs to God's holy people, who live in the light. <u>For he has rescued us from the one who rules in the kingdom of darkness, and he has brought us into the Kingdom of his dear Son.</u> (Colossians 1:9-13)(NLT)

Once you are saved, you are free from Satan's control. You are not subject to his evil manipulation. You are destined for Heaven. You live on this Earth until your body wears out, then you go to Heaven, your eternal destination. When Christians die, many times we say they "went home to be with the Lord." We say that because Heaven is home for a Christian.

For our citizenship is in heaven... (Philippians 3:20)

Even though Heaven is a future destination, we should learn to live by the principles of the Kingdom of God now. Unfortunately, Satan still tries to deceive Christians into believing he is in control of their lives. You no longer are subject to him and should reject his attempts to control you. Consider this scenario. You are in church one Sunday morning and a man dressed in a Chinese military uniform walks in the back door, down the aisle and stands at the front of the church. He begins to shout and say, "This church must shut down! There is no God! No more prayer! No more preaching about Jesus!" Would you expect your pastor to tell everyone to leave, turn out the lights, lock the doors and say, "Well, I guess that's the end of this church!?" Would you stop believing in God and stop praying? Of course not! This man represents the country of China. This is America. We are not subject to the laws of China. We don't have to obey his orders, no matter how loud he shouts or how much he threatens to lock us up. He has no authority here.

The same attitude should prevail when Satan fires thoughts into your head that are contrary to God's word. Satan may shout into your mind and say, "You will never overcome your addiction to pornography! You are a loser and your marriage will end in divorce just like your last one! This sickness will kill you! Your financial problems will cause you to lose your house, your cars and your job!" Don't pay any attention to those attempts to intimidate you. You are no longer subject to Satan's control because you no longer are a citizen of the kingdom of darkness.

> *Therefore submit to God. Resist the devil and he will flee from you. (James 4:7)*

In order to overcome Satan, you must resist him. In order to resist him, you have to know what is from God and what is from the Devil. If you are confused about the two kingdoms, you may find yourself resisting God and submitting to the Devil instead of the other way around. The Devil will only flee from you if you resist him. You have to learn to <u>resist</u> everything that is part of the kingdom of darkness and <u>submit</u> to everything that is part of the kingdom of God.

> *Be careful! Watch out for attacks from the Devil, your great enemy. He prowls around like a roaring lion, looking for some victim to devour. Take a firm stand against him, and be strong in your faith. Remember that your Christian brothers and sisters all over the world are going through the same kind of suffering you are. (1 Peter 5:8-9)(NLT)*

Satan is like a hungry lion, constantly on the prowl. He is looking for prey he can conquer. He has to look for prey because everyone is not a good target. Those who know about his tactics will resist him. Those who do not know the difference between God's kingdom and Satan's kingdom are easy targets.

Satan is our enemy. He wants to thwart God's plans from being accomplished in people's lives and in the world. This is critical to understand. Some have made statements in the midst of tragedy such as this, "Everything happens for a reason. We don't know why this happened, but God has a plan." The implication in this kind of statement is that God either caused the tragedy or allowed it to happen as part of His divine plan. I challenge you to consider if that line of reasoning is consistent with Scripture. We are not in Heaven yet. <u>Everything that happens in this world is not God's will</u>. Satan is still active here. People make bad decisions contrary to God's will. Be careful about blaming God for horrible events.

Here are a few examples for you to consider. Were any of these God's will? Did God "allow" them to happen because it was part of His plan?

- Adam and Eve ate the fruit of the knowledge of good and evil.
- Cain committed the first murder when he killed his brother Abel.
- Abraham Lincoln was assassinated.
- Adolph Hitler murdered thousands of Jews in the Holocaust.
- Timothy McVeigh blew up a federal building in Oklahoma City, murdering innocent adults and children.
- Terrorists hijacked and crashed four planes on 9-11-01, killing thousands of innocent people.
- Innocent children have been kidnapped, sexually molested and some were killed.

None of those were part of God's plan. I know they were not because they fulfill Satan's mission described in *John 10:10* to "steal, kill and destroy" and go against God's word. Satan is still able to influence people to do terrible, evil acts. That is why it is important to know the difference between the two kingdoms. We must always be ready and willing to resist the Devil's attempts to influence or control us. Even the Apostle Paul had to deal with constant attacks from the enemy. Paul had received supernatural revelation about Jesus and all that He accomplished during His time on Earth. Paul was working hard to spread this gospel message to as many people as possible. Although Paul preached a wonderful message of grace and freedom, nearly everywhere he went he encountered severe opposition. Who do you think wanted to keep the message of Jesus from spreading? Satan, of course. Satan wants to keep people from hearing about Jesus. He wants to keep people in his kingdom of darkness. So Satan assigned a demon spirit to follow Paul and stir up as much trouble as possible. Paul referred to this demon spirit in a figurative way as a "thorn in the flesh." A thorn in the flesh is a constant irritant. This demon spirit was a constant irritant to Paul.

> *And lest I should be exalted above measure by the abundance of the revelations, a <u>thorn in the flesh</u> was given to me, a <u>messenger of Satan</u> to buffet me, lest I be exalted above measure. (2 Corinthians 12:7)*

The Greek word translated "messenger" in this Scripture is "angelos.' This word is translated as "angel" 181 of 188 times it is found in the New Testament. The remaining seven times it is translated as "messenger." Since Paul describes this "angelos" or "angel" as being from Satan, it seems clear he is referring to a demon spirit. Paul had to learn to resist this demon the same way you and I have to learn to resist demons. The first step is to recognize the source of the problem. A lack of understanding about what is from God and what is from Satan can cause you to be defeated in your daily walk.

> *My people are destroyed for lack of knowledge. ...(Hosea 4:6)*

Learning to recognize the difference between the two kingdoms requires learning to think differently. Satan tries his best to control people and events on the Earth. He wants to influence the way you think, also. That is why you have to work to align your thinking with God. If you allow it to happen, you will learn to think like Satan instead of God. Satan wants you to conform to his way of thinking.

> *And do not be conformed to this world, but be transformed by the renewing of your mind, that you may prove what is that good and acceptable and perfect will of God. (Romans 12:2)*

You have to renew your mind because it gets polluted with worldly opinions. A constant diet of R-rated movies and perverse television programs can corrupt your thinking to align with Satan. You are transformed into a person who knows the will of God by putting God's thoughts into your mind on a regular basis. God's thoughts are found in His word, the Bible. Regular Bible reading and listening to anointed Bible teachers will help you keep your mind renewed. Then you will be able to recognize the difference between God's thoughts and Satan's thoughts.

CURSES AND BLESSINGS

Under God's Old Testament system, obedience produced the blessing of God and disobedience produced curses. Another word for disobedience is "sin." Sin brought on the curse. When Jesus died on the cross, He became sin for us. He took sin and <u>the result of sin</u> away. The result of sin was separation from God, but it was also the curses described in the Old Testament laws. When Jesus bled and died on the cross, <u>He took sin and its results, the curse</u>.

> *Christ has redeemed us from the curse of the law, having become a curse for us (for it is written, "Cursed is everyone who hangs on a tree"), that the blessing of Abraham might come upon the Gentiles in Christ Jesus, that we might receive the promise of the Spirit through faith. (Galatians 3:13-14)*

We know Jesus took sin away so we no longer have to be controlled by sin. We know we should resist sin because it is not from God and Jesus has freed us from sin's power. The same is true of the curse. Jesus took the curse away and now we should resist the curse. We resist it because it is part of the kingdom of Satan and Jesus has delivered us from the effects of the curses. The blessings are ours because we now identify with Jesus. Jesus frees us from the results of sin and gives us the benefits of the blessings. You can stay free from the results of the curse by eliminating sin from your life. You eliminate sin by making choices to obey God and His word. If you make a mistake and sin, repent immediately and ask God for forgiveness. Jesus will forgive you and you will stay in the realm of blessings instead of curses.

When you renew your mind with an understanding of the blessings and curses, you can better understand what to submit to and what to resist. God's description of the blessings and curses is found in the Old Testament book of Deuteronomy. In the following pages, I describe a few of the different categories of blessings and curses. Remember that <u>because of Jesus, we can live free from the curses and enjoy the benefits of the blessings</u>.

FINANCIAL PROSPERITY

Take the time to read all of this Scripture. This now applies to you because of Jesus.

> *"Now it shall come to pass, if you diligently obey the voice of the LORD your God, to observe carefully all His commandments which I command you today, that the LORD your God will set you high above all nations of the earth. "And all these blessings shall come upon you and overtake you, because you obey the voice of the LORD your God: "Blessed shall you be in the city, and blessed shall you be in the country. "Blessed shall be the fruit of your body, the produce of your ground and the increase of your herds, the increase of your cattle and the offspring of your flocks. "Blessed shall be your basket and your kneading bowl.*
>
> *"Blessed shall you be when you come in, and blessed shall you be when you go out. "The LORD will cause your enemies who rise against you to be defeated before your face; they shall come out against you one way and flee before you seven ways. "The LORD will command the blessing on you in your storehouses and in all to which you set your hand, and He will bless you in the land which the LORD your God is giving you. "The LORD will establish you as a holy people to Himself, just as He has sworn to you, if you keep the commandments of the*

LORD your God and walk in His ways. "Then all peoples of the earth shall see that you are called by the name of the LORD, and they shall be afraid of you. "And the LORD will grant you plenty of goods, in the fruit of your body, in the increase of your livestock, and in the produce of your ground, in the land of which the LORD swore to your fathers to give you. "The LORD will open to you His good treasure, the heavens, to give the rain to your land in its season, and to bless all the work of your hand. You shall lend to many nations, but you shall not borrow. "And the LORD will make you the head and not the tail; you shall be above only, and not be beneath, if you heed the commandments of the LORD your God, which I command you today, and are careful to observe them. "So you shall not turn aside from any of the words which I command you this day, to the right or the left, to go after other gods to serve them. (Deuteronomy 28:1-14)

This is written in the context of life as it was thousands of years ago. These people made their living off the "produce of the ground," the "increase of their herds and cattle," and food they prepared and ate from their crops and animals. They had "storehouses" where they kept their food and valuables. You may not live off the food in your garden or have livestock or a literal storehouse. If this description of the blessings of God were written today, it would probably talk about the increase of your sales and investments. Instead of a "storehouse" it would refer to your checking or money market account. The point is this: Whatever you set your hand to do within the will of God for your life will prosper because of the blessing of God. Instead of being at the bottom of the organizational chart at work, you can move up according to your unique abilities. Instead of going out of business, you can see your business grow and prosper in response to your effort and aptitude. The blessings are part of God's kingdom. Believing and expecting promotion and financial increase in your life is part of "submitting to God."

> *Therefore submit to God. Resist the devil and he will flee from you. (James 4:7)*

The curses are the opposite of the blessings. Don't submit to the curses. The curses are part of Satan's kingdom and should be resisted just like you would resist sin.

> *"But it shall come to pass, if you do not obey the voice of the LORD your God, to observe carefully all His commandments and His statutes which I command you today, that all these curses will come upon you and overtake you: "Cursed shall you be in the city, and cursed shall you be in the country. "Cursed shall be your basket and your kneading bowl. "Cursed shall be the fruit of your body and the produce of your land, the increase of your cattle and the offspring of your flocks. "Cursed shall you be when you come in, and cursed shall you be when you go out. (Deuteronomy 28:15-19)*

Many business people agonize daily over the state of their financial affairs. They may have trouble sleeping because of worry over the sales figures or overhead costs or a new competitor. When you prosper according to God's principles, you can live a life of peace. You can sleep at night knowing that your prosperity came from the hand of God. You can live a life of joy instead of sorrow when you recognize your success comes from God. When you obtain prosperity by following God's principles and trusting Him, you don't have to worry about the future.

> *The blessing of the LORD makes one rich, And He adds no sorrow with it. (Proverbs 10:22)*

DIVINE HEALTH AND HEALING

Sickness and disease came into the Earth because of sin. If Adam and Eve had never sinned, they would still be physically alive and healthy today. Sickness came into the world because of the author of sin, Satan. Sickness is a corruption of the health God originally created. If you are sick with a sinus infection, it doesn't necessarily mean you have a demon in your nose. However, sickness is in the world due to the corruption brought about by sin. <u>Sickness is part of the curse of sin and should be resisted and not welcomed</u>. I have picked out several Scriptures referring to sickness as a part of the curse of the law:

> *"But it shall come to pass, if you do not obey the voice of the LORD your God, to observe carefully all His commandments and His statutes which I command you today, that all these curses will come upon you and overtake you: (Deuteronomy 28:15)*

> *"The LORD will make the plague cling to you until He has consumed you from the land which you are going to possess. "The LORD will strike you with consumption, with fever, with inflammation, with severe burning fever, with the sword, with scorching, and with mildew; they shall pursue you until you perish. (Deuteronomy 28:21-22)*

> *"The LORD will strike you with the boils of Egypt, with tumors, with the scab, and with the itch, from which you cannot be healed. "The LORD will strike you with madness and blindness and confusion of heart. (Deuteronomy 28:27-28)*

> *"The LORD will strike you in the knees and on the legs with severe boils which cannot be healed, and from the sole of your foot to the top of your head. (Deuteronomy 28:35)*

> *"then the LORD will bring upon you and your descendants extraordinary plagues—great and prolonged plagues—and serious and prolonged*

sicknesses. "Moreover He will bring back on you all the diseases of Egypt, of which you were afraid, and they shall cling to you. "Also every sickness and every plague, which is not written in this Book of the Law, will the LORD bring upon you until you are destroyed. (Deuteronomy 28:59-61)

God provided health and healing under the Old Covenant for those who chose to serve and obey Him. God's plan was for everybody to live out their lives until their appointed time to die arrived.

"So you shall serve the LORD your God, and He will bless your bread and your water. And I will take sickness away from the midst of you. "No one shall suffer miscarriage or be barren in your land; I will fulfill the number of your days. (Exodus 23:25-26)

Jesus established a New Covenant. This New Covenant is better than the Old. It is better because it contains all the blessings of the Old Covenant, but adds more! The New Covenant includes the New Birth and the presence of the Holy Spirit living in you at all times. The New Covenant adds a way to be free from the guilt of sin. The New Covenant makes a way for Christians to know they will go directly to Heaven when they die. The Old Covenant promises of health and healing are included in the New Covenant.

But now He has obtained a more excellent ministry, inasmuch as He is also Mediator of a better covenant, which was established on better promises. (Hebrews 8:6)

Jesus demonstrated the will of God when He walked on the Earth. Peter preached a wonderful sermon one day to a house full of people yearning to learn more about God. Part of what Peter said about Jesus during this powerful sermon is shown in this Scripture:

"how God anointed Jesus of Nazareth with the Holy Spirit and with power, who went about doing good and healing all who were oppressed by the devil, for God was with Him. (Acts 10:38)

Peter explains clearly that Jesus was anointed by God to do the things He did. He also describes healing as something good. Then he says Jesus healed people who were oppressed by the Devil. That fits with what we have been studying. Sickness is part of the oppression in the world caused by sin and Satan, the author of sin. Sickness is part of Satan's kingdom. Christians have been delivered from Satan's kingdom and should resist everything from the Devil's kingdom.

Some have felt God has a purpose in making people sick, or allowing them to be sick to teach them a lesson. I spoke with a man one time whose wife was very sick. I asked him if I could come and pray for her healing. This man refused my offer of prayer. When I asked him why I could not pray for her, he said, "Because it might not be God's will for her to be healed." This made no sense to me. He willingly took his wife to a doctor. He followed the instructions of the doctor. He filled the medical prescriptions given to her by the doctor. He did all these things because he wanted his wife to get well. This puzzled me. If God may not want her to get well, why take her to the doctor? If God doesn't want her well, aren't you fighting against the will of God by taking your prescriptions? God can bring wholeness to a person through a variety of ways such as prayer, spiritual gifts, medicine, surgery, nutritional therapy, alternative medicine, etc. If he was concerned that it might not be God's will to heal her, then he shouldn't have done anything for her!

FEAR AND WORRY

Fear and worry are from the kingdom of darkness. These two cousins are not sent from God. Since you are no longer in Satan's kingdom, you should resist fear and worry like you would resist sin. Worry is expecting the worst to happen. Faith believes God's best plan for you will play out. Faith and fear are opposites. Look at what

Jesus said to His disciples when they were afraid a storm was going to cause their death.

> *But He said to them, "Why are you so fearful? How is it that you have no faith?" (Mark 4:40)*

Do you see how Jesus described fear and faith as opposites? He said if you are **full** of fear, you have **no** faith. Full of fear = no faith. The opposite is also true. Full of faith = no fear. Faith comes from believing God's word is true. Faith is the way God wants you to live when you are a Christian *(...The just shall live by faith. - Romans 1:17)*. Drive out fear by increasing your faith. Increase your faith by increasing your intake of the word of God *(So then faith comes by hearing, and hearing by the word of God. – Romans 10:17)*.

> *Don't worry about anything; instead, pray about everything. Tell God what you need, and thank him for all he has done. If you do this, you will experience God's peace, which is far more wonderful than the human mind can understand. His peace will guard your hearts and minds as you live in Christ Jesus. (Philippians 4:6-7)(NLT)*

Peace, the opposite of fear, comes when you trust God for the help you need. Replace fear with peace by remembering and speaking God's promises for your every need. When worry and fear come knocking at your door, answer it with God's word and they will run away, leaving you with the peace of God.

STRIFE

Strife is defined as, "bitter, often violent dissension or conflict." God dislikes strife. God likes harmony. God likes it when people are "on the same page." Some people thrive on arguments. Some folks love conflict and controversy. If it doesn't occur naturally, they will start a conflict just because they love it so much. Have you ever known anyone like that? Sometimes we say to those people, "You would argue with a fence post!"

> *But avoid foolish and ignorant disputes, knowing*
> *that they generate strife. And a servant of the Lord*
> *must not quarrel but be gentle to all, able to teach,*
> *patient, in humility correcting those who are in*
> *opposition, if God perhaps will grant them repen-*
> *tance, so that they may know the truth, and that*
> *they may come to their senses and escape the snare*
> *of the devil, having been taken captive by him to do*
> *his will. (2 Timothy 2:23-26)*

Strife and contention are part of the kingdom of darkness. You have been delivered from Satan's kingdom of darkness. You should resist strife and contention like you would resist someone trying to kidnap your child.

> *Now I urge you, brethren, <u>note those</u> who cause divi-*
> *sions and offenses, contrary to the doctrine which*
> *you learned, and <u>avoid them</u>. (Romans 16:17)*

The Bible says to notice people who regularly cause arguments that result in hurt feelings. Once you have identified people who are like that, you should <u>avoid them</u> as much as possible. You may have to end a friendship to eliminate strife and division in your life. You may have to stop going to lunch with a troublemaker who constantly complains and tries to get you to join in his hurtful game. Don't allow yourself to venture into Satan's kingdom of division.

> *Now I plead with you, brethren, by the name of our*
> *Lord Jesus Christ, that you all speak the same thing,*
> *and that there be <u>no divisions</u> among you, but that*
> *you be perfectly joined together in the same mind*
> *and in the same judgment. (1 Corinthians 1:10)*

Nobody is going to be an exact clone of you with the exact same opinions on every topic. However, differing opinions should not result in violent arguments and hurt feelings. You need to find a church home where your beliefs match up with the pastor who is feeding you the word of God each week. You don't need to be in violent disagreement with the church doctrine where you attend. Constant quarrels and bickering among Christians is a sign of spiritual immaturity.

> *Dear brothers and sisters, when I was with you I couldn't talk to you as I would to mature Christians. I had to talk as though you belonged to this world or as though you were infants in the Christian life. I had to feed you with milk and not with solid food, because you couldn't handle anything stronger. And you still aren't ready, for you are still controlled by your own sinful desires. You are jealous of one another and quarrel with each other. Doesn't that prove you are controlled by your own desires? You are acting like people who don't belong to the Lord. (1 Corinthians 3:1-3)(NLT)*

Paul was writing to the Christians in the city of Corinth and he compared their behavior to that of babies. He said they needed to grow up. He said he had to feed them milk instead of solid food. What would you think if you went to a Wednesday night church supper at a new church and the tables all had baby bottles on them? What if you walked in and saw the leaders of that church sucking on baby bottles? You would think, "something is terribly wrong here," wouldn't you?

This is what Paul was saying. He told them he could tell they were still babies because of their constant quarreling. Unfortunately, this describes many churches today. Some are controlled by the babies who cry the loudest when they don't get their way. They want their bottle and they want the milk to be just the right temperature to suit them. Babies think the world revolves around them and what they want. Baby Christians think their pastor should make them feel good all the time or they will throw a tantrum until they get their way. This should not be the case among leaders in a church. These people may be Christians, but they are still living in Satan's kingdom because of their immature jealousies and love of fights.

GOD'S WORD

The Devil does not like the word of God. Satan will do anything within his power to keep God's word from producing in your life. Jesus told a parable to illustrate this truth. The parable described a farmer who planted seeds. Some of the seed landed on the hardened path and was eaten immediately by the birds before it had a chance to grow at all. Some seed fell on stony ground and did not produce any lasting effect because of a lack of root structure. Some of the seed was scattered among thorns which choked the young plant and did not allow it to get the nutrients necessary for growth. Other seed, however, fell on good soil and produced a great harvest. Jesus explained the parable as being about the word of God and its possible effect in a person's life:

> *The farmer I talked about is the one who brings God's message to others. The seed that fell on the hard path represents those who hear the message, but then Satan comes at once and takes it away from them. The rocky soil represents those who hear the message and receive it with joy. But like young plants in such soil, their roots don't go very deep. At first they get along fine, but they wilt as soon as they have problems or are persecuted because they believe the word. The thorny ground represents those who hear and accept the Good News, but all too quickly the message is crowded out by the cares of this life, the lure of wealth, and the desire for nice things, so no crop is produced. But the good soil represents those who hear and accept God's message and produce a huge harvest—thirty,*

sixty, or even a hundred times as much as had been planted." (Mark 4:14-20)(NLT)

Notice it is the Devil who wants to keep the word of God from producing any fruit in your life. Satan "comes at once" to take the seed of God's word once it is planted. Have you ever had the Devil fire thoughts into your head after church? Maybe he says things to you like, "You don't really believe you can be free from guilt, do you?" Or, "God doesn't really want to heal you. That stuff was only for Bible days!" Satan is "coming at once" to steal the word that was planted in your heart.

Or perhaps you hear the word of God about His financial provision. You get excited and full of joy about paying off some debt and increasing your giving to missionary work in other countries. Then Satan sends some "persecution" your way to see if you really believe what you have heard. Maybe your washing machine goes out or your air conditioner needs a new compressor. Do you still increase your giving or do you wilt under the Satanic oppression?

Others hear the word of God and believe it. They commit to live for God and put Him first in everything they do. But things get busy at work and they decide Sunday mornings are good days to go into the office and get a lot done without interruptions. Or maybe they reason they can find some good buys at flea markets on weekends. Or they have to go work out every morning and no longer have time to read the Bible or pray. Or they have too many TV programs to watch each week and prayer with their spouse is no longer possible.

Satan wants you to be too busy to spend time with God. He knows that time with God in prayer and in the word of God produces faith. And increased faith enables you to resist and overcome the Devil. Satan knows he must keep the word of God from producing faith in your life because your faith will give you victory over the world system that Satan works diligently to control.

For whatever is born of God overcomes the world. And this is the victory that has overcome the world— our faith. Who is he who overcomes the world,

but he who believes that Jesus is the Son of God?
(1 John 5:4-5)

RESIST SATAN'S KINGDOM

I could continue to give examples of the differences between the kingdom of God and the kingdom of darkness. However, I will stop with these and leave you with this admonition. Do not put yourself in a place where Satan operates. When you travel, you wouldn't check your family into a motel in a high-crime area of town with drug dealers and prostitutes in the rooms on either side of you. Stay away from Satan's turf. Don't give him an opportunity to gain control of any part of your life. Resist him.

"Be angry, and do not sin": do not let the sun go
down on your wrath, <u>nor give place to the devil</u>.
(Ephesians 4:26-27)

Look at what Jesus said. He gives you a guide to determine if something is from God or from the Devil. Then you will know whether to resist it because it is from Satan or submit to it because it is from God.

"The thief does not come except to steal, and to
kill, and to destroy. I have come that they may have
life, and that they may have it more abundantly.
(John 10:10)

Satan tries to steal, kill and destroy. Sickness tries to steal your money, your time and your ability to actively serve God. Resist it. Sin brings guilt and confusion. Resist it. Fear brings worry and lack of peace. Resist it.

God wants you to have an abundant life in every area. Having an abundance of money frees you from debt and allows you to give freely to God and those in need. Submit to it. Healing allows you to take care of yourself or your family and serve God freely. Submit to it. Confession and forgiveness brings a cleansing of the conscience and freedom from guilt. Submit to it.

Anything that steals, kills or destroys comes from Satan. Resist it. Anything that produces abundant life comes from God. Submit to it.

CHAPTER 11

EXERCISING YOUR AUTHORITY

W e have studied the theology behind your authority over the
Devil. Now it is time to put that information to use! This
book is much more than an interesting Bible study. The purpose of
the book is to enable you to live in victory over the schemes of the
Devil. Let's review a few of the basic truths we have uncovered.
Then we will learn how to translate those truths into action.

> *And I will put enmity Between you and the woman,*
> *And between your seed and her Seed; He shall*
> *bruise your head, And you shall bruise His heel."*
> *(Genesis 3:15)*

After Adam and Eve sinned, God told Satan that the "Seed"
would take back the authority that Satan had usurped from man.

> *Then the Angel of the LORD called to Abraham a*
> *second time out of heaven, and said: "By Myself I*
> *have sworn, says the LORD, because you have done*
> *this thing, and have not withheld your son, your only*
> *son— "blessing I will bless you, and multiplying I*
> *will multiply your descendants as the stars of the*
> *heaven and as the sand which is on the seashore;*
> *and your descendants shall possess the gate of*

their enemies. "In your seed all the nations of the earth shall be blessed, because you have obeyed My voice." (Genesis 22:15-18)

After Abraham demonstrated his willingness to obey the terms of the covenant, an angel delivered a message from God to Abraham. God told Abraham his seed would control the domain of his enemies.

Now to Abraham and his Seed were the promises made. He does not say, "And to seeds," as of many, but as of one, "And to your Seed," who is Christ. (Galatians 3:16)

And if you are Christ's, then you are Abraham's seed, and heirs according to the promise. (Galatians 3:29)

Jesus was the "Seed" to whom the promises were made. We now have a right to the promise of controlling Satan's domain because we belong to Jesus Christ.

giving thanks to the Father who has qualified us to be partakers of the inheritance of the saints in the light. He has delivered us from the power of dark-ness and conveyed us into the kingdom of the Son of His love, (Colossians 1:12-13)

We have been delivered from the authority of Satan. Jesus took care of that with His death, burial and resurrection. Now we must exercise our authority.

All over America, police academies regularly graduate new police officers. Their training is complete. They have passed all the required tests. They are given a badge to represent their newly acquired authority. Yet, criminals continue to commit crimes. Don't they know that law enforcement officials have authority over them? Don't they know they can be arrested and their illegal activities stopped? Of course they know that. Criminals will continue to commit crimes and force law enforcement officers to demonstrate their authority. Most criminals won't stop until they are arrested.

The same is true of Satan. He knows believers have authority over him. He knows the name of Jesus is above him and anything he can bring your way. Yet he continues to try to influence people for evil. He won't stop trying to hinder you. You have to <u>use</u> the authority you have as a Christian.

OPPOSITION IS NORMAL

It is not a sin to be tempted. It is not a sin to be tempted repeatedly. The Devil tempted Jesus. Most people think Satan only bothered Jesus with the three temptations described in the Bible when He was in the wilderness fasting for 40 days.

> *Then Jesus, being filled with the Holy Spirit, returned from the Jordan and was led by the Spirit into the wilderness, <u>being tempted for forty days by the devil</u>. And in those days He ate nothing, and afterward, when they had ended, He was hungry. (Luke 4:1-2)*

> *Now when the devil had ended every temptation, he departed from Him <u>until an opportune time</u>. (Luke 4:13)*

Jesus was tempted for the entire 40 days He was in the wilderness. We only have a record of the final three temptations. After Jesus successfully resisted Satan the final three times, Satan left Him. But he only left until another opportunity arose to bring more temptations. Jesus had to deal with the Devil all His life on Earth.

The Devil will attack you repeatedly, also. You will have to learn to resist him on a regular basis. <u>Learning to resist the Devil should be a normal part of the Christian life</u>. Satan desperately wants to stop God's plans from being fulfilled on the Earth.

Be sober, be vigilant; because your adversary the devil walks about like a roaring lion, seeking whom he may devour. Resist him, steadfast in the faith, knowing that the same sufferings are experienced by your brotherhood in the world. (1 Peter 5:8-9)

The Devil is referred to as our "adversary." An adversary is one who opposes you. Satan is against you. He looks for people he "may devour." That means he can't devour anybody he wants. He has to look for people who will allow him to have his way in their life. If you resist him, Satan will flee from you. If you try to ignore him, the Devil will control your life as much as possible. He tries to cause problems for everybody at one time or another. That is why having problems in life is not necessarily a sign that you are out of the will of God. Even the Apostle Paul, after he committed his life to Jesus, had continual problems caused by Satan.

Dear brothers and sisters, after we were separated from you for a little while (though our hearts never left you), we tried very hard to come back because of our intense longing to see you again. We wanted very much to come, and I, Paul, tried again and again, but Satan prevented us. (1 Thessalonians 2:17-18)(NLT)

USING YOUR AUTHORITY

Adam had authority over the Devil. He was supposed to guard the Garden of Eden by using the authority God had given him (*Genesis 2:15*). Adam allowed Satan to come into the Garden of Eden and visit with Eve. Adam could have ordered Satan to leave, but he didn't. Bad things happened because Adam refused to use the authority God had given him.

In Old Testament times, God made promises to His people, the nation of Israel. God used Moses to deliver them from slavery in Egypt. With mighty miracles, God finally forced Pharaoh to release the Israelites. Moses led them out of Egypt and, with another incredible miracle, through the Red Sea to complete their escape from Pharaoh. God told them He was giving them a land called Canaan, a land of abundance, flowing with milk and honey. This was to be their ultimate destination.

> *"For if you carefully keep all these command-ments which I command you to do—to love the* LORD *your God, to walk in all His ways, and to hold fast to Him— "then the* LORD *will drive out all these nations from before you, and* you will dispos-sess *greater and mightier nations than yourselves. "Every place on which the sole of your foot treads shall be yours: from the wilderness and Lebanon, from the river, the River Euphrates, even to the Western Sea, shall be your territory. "No man shall be able to stand against you; the* LORD *your God will put the dread of you and the fear of you upon all the land where you tread, just as He has said to you. (Deuteronomy 11:22-25)*

> *"For* you will cross over the Jordan and go in to possess the land *which the* LORD *your God is giving you, and you will possess it and dwell in it. (Deuteronomy 11:31)*

God told His people they would have to drive the people out of the land He gave them. God said they would have to "possess the land." That meant forcibly take possession of the land. It meant exercising the authority God had given them to drive out everyone living on their new land. When the Israelites got close to their new homeland, Moses sent out spies to see what the land looked like and to size up their enemies.

> *The* LORD *now said to Moses, "Send men to explore the land of Canaan, the land I am giving to Israel. Send one leader from each of the twelve ancestral tribes." (Numbers 13:1-2)(NLT)*

*Moses gave the men these instructions as he sent
them out to explore the land: "Go northward through
the Negev into the hill country. See what the land is
like and find out whether the people living there are
strong or weak, few or many. What kind of land do
they live in? Is it good or bad? Do their towns have
walls or are they unprotected? How is the soil? Is
it fertile or poor? Are there many trees? Enter the
land boldly, and bring back samples of the crops you
see." (It happened to be the season for harvesting
the first ripe grapes.) (Numbers 13:17-20)(NLT)*

The spies were gone over a month. When they returned, Moses
and Aaron and the entire nation eagerly awaited their report.

*After exploring the land for forty days, the men
returned to Moses, Aaron, and the people of
Israel at Kadesh in the wilderness of Paran. They
reported to the whole community what they had
seen and showed them the fruit they had taken
from the land. This was their report to Moses:
"We arrived in the land you sent us to see, and it
is indeed a magnificent country—a land flowing
with milk and honey. Here is some of its fruit as
proof. (Numbers 13:25-27)(NLT)*

The report came back that the land was wonderful. It was fertile
and produced magnificent crops. If they had stopped the report there,
things would have been so much better! But they did not stop there.
Remember, God told them the people in this country were "greater
and mightier nations." But God said He would go before them and
"no man shall be able to stand against you." Sadly, ten of the twelve
spies refused to believe the promise of God. They focused on the
strength of their enemies.

*But the people living there are powerful, and their
cities and towns are fortified and very large. We*

also saw the descendants of Anak who are living there! The Amalekites live in the Negev, and the Hittites, Jebusites, and Amorites live in the hill country. The Canaanites live along the coast of the Mediterranean Sea and along the Jordan Valley." (Numbers 13:28-29)(NLT)

Caleb and Joshua were the only two spies who chose to believe God would do what He said He would do. Caleb attempted to persuade the people to take the land God had given them. But the others stood their ground with their evil report. The report was evil because it was in opposition to God's report.

But Caleb tried to encourage the people as they stood before Moses. "Let's go at once to take the land," he said. "We can certainly conquer it!" But the other men who had explored the land with him answered, "We can't go up against them! They are stronger than we are!" So they spread discouraging reports about the land among the Israelites: "The land we explored will swallow up any who go to live there. All the people we saw were huge. We even saw giants there, the descendants of Anak. We felt like grasshoppers next to them, and that's what we looked like to them!" (Numbers 13:30-33)(NLT)

It is amazing, but ten people instilled enough fear in an entire nation to persuade them to ignore the promises of God. They quickly forgot the guarantee of victory God had given them. They even wanted to fire Moses as their leader and go back to the harsh bondage of slavery in Egypt.

Then all the people began weeping aloud, and they cried all night. Their voices rose in a great chorus of complaint against Moses and Aaron. "We wish we had died in Egypt, or even here in the wilder-ness!" they wailed. "Why is the LORD taking us to this country only to have us die in battle? Our wives and little ones will be carried off as slaves! Let's get out of here and return to Egypt!" Then they plotted among themselves, "Let's choose a leader and go back to Egypt!" (Numbers 14:1-4)(NLT)

Moses and Aaron immediately began to pray for the children of Israel. Joshua and Caleb tried again to encourage the people to remember and believe God's promises.

Then Moses and Aaron fell face down on the ground before the people of Israel. Two of the men who had explored the land, Joshua son of Nun and Caleb son of Jephunneh, tore their clothing. They said to the community of Israel, "The land we explored is a wonderful land! And if the LORD is pleased with us, he will bring us safely into that land and give it to us. It is a rich land flowing with milk and honey, and he will give it to us! Do not rebel against the LORD, and don't be afraid of the people of the land. They are only helpless prey to us! They have no protection, but the LORD is with us! Don't be afraid of them!" (Numbers 14:5-9)(NLT)

Many Old Testament stories can help us on two levels. There are the lessons we can learn from the events as they occurred. Then there are other lessons we can learn by applying the principles to our life under the New Testament. Many Old Testament events are called "types and shadows" because they are pictures of New Testament truths.

Some have taught that Egypt is a type of sin and that Canaan is a type of Heaven. I believe that is only partially accurate. Canaan had many enemies who had to be removed. Heaven has no enemies we will have to cast out. It is true that Egypt is a representation of sin. Before you are born again, you are enslaved by the Devil, just as the nation of Israel was in slavery in Egypt. The Red Sea represents the born again experience, deliverance from the kingdom of darkness.

But Canaan represents the abundant life Jesus promised us we could live on Earth after we are saved. We have spiritual enemies on Earth -- Satan and his demons. Our authority over the Devil and demons is to be exercised now, in this life. We won't need to cast out any demons when we are in Heaven. To the nation of Israel, Canaan was the "Promised Land." To the New Testament believer, Canaan represents the "Land of Promises!" God has provided many wonderful promises for the believer. Satan is our adversary and wants to stop us from living in the reality of God's promises.

Most of the nation of Israel refused to resist the enemy. They could have immediately conquered Canaan and obtained everything God promised. But they refused to fight the enemy. The same is true of many believers today. God has given us authority over the Devil. If we will use the authority God has given us, we can drive Satan and demons out of our lives.

> *Therefore submit to God. Resist the devil and he will flee from you. (James 4:7)*

Resist the Devil and he will run away from you. Refuse to resist the Devil and he will regularly disrupt your life. I remember being in a Bible study class in a church I pastored. A lady began to describe how her young son would wake up in the night, terrified and crying out for his mother. I recognized the work of the Devil immediately. Fear and terror are part of the kingdom of darkness ruled by Satan.

> *You shall not be afraid of the terror by night...*
> *(Psalm 91:5)*

I briefly explained how she must take authority over the Devil and the terror he was bringing to her son in the night. I asked her to put into action what I had just taught her. She began to pray and ask God to keep the Devil away from her son. I gently stopped her and explained this truth again. I said, "You must take authority over the Devil. God has given you the responsibility to cast that demon of terror out of your son's life. You have to talk to the Devil and tell him your son is off limits." She then began to rebuke Satan and tell him to leave her son alone. I told her to continue to do this because the Devil is stubborn and also to teach her son how to do it. The terror attacks began to diminish and eventually disappeared because of this mother's willingness to exercise her authority over Satan and his demons.

WEAPONS FOR BATTLE

Most people resist conflict. However, I must tell you the truth. <u>Conflict with Satan is inevitable.</u> You need to be properly equipped to fight against him. Weapons are necessary to subdue the enemy. Soldiers must be outfitted with both offensive and defensive equipment before they go into battle. Christians also need both offensive and defensive weapons to battle the forces of darkness. Weapons are used for warfare.

> *For though we walk in the flesh, we do not war according to the flesh. For the weapons of our warfare are not carnal but mighty in God for pulling down strongholds, casting down arguments and every high thing that exalts itself against the knowledge of God, bringing every thought into captivity to the obedience of Christ, (2 Corinthians 10:3-5)*

The weapons we use to defeat Satan are not ones that are readily visible to our physical senses (the flesh). But they are mightier than anything you have ever seen a soldier use because they are from God. Paul talked about going to war against the forces of darkness with the proper equipment.

> *A final word: Be strong with the Lord's mighty power. (Ephesians 6:10)(NLT)*

We are strong when we depend on the power of God and not our own strength.

Put on all of God's armor so that you will be able to stand firm against all strategies and tricks of the Devil. (Ephesians 6:11)(NLT)

Part of the armor isn't enough. We must wear all of it in order to successfully and consistently defeat the Devil.

For we are not fighting against people made of flesh and blood, but against the evil rulers and authorities of the unseen world, against those mighty powers of darkness who rule this world, and against wicked spirits in the heavenly realms. (Ephesians 6:12)(NLT)

We wrestle with demon spirits, not people. We battle the spiritual forces controlling people and circumstances. That is why spiritual warfare should be a normal part of your life.

Use every piece of God's armor to resist the enemy in the time of evil, so that after the battle you will still be standing firm. (Ephesians 6:13)(NLT)

After we have done everything the Bible says to do, we continue to stand firm, resisting the Devil, until we see the victory manifested. When you choose to resist the Devil, it may not look at first as if anything is changing. The Devil is stubborn, so you have to be persistent and not give up. You have to continue to use the name of Jesus and command the enemy to leave your marriage, your finances, your workplace, wherever he is causing problems. <u>If you keep the force of faith applied, you will eventually win because the word of God says you will.</u>

You are of God, little children, and have overcome them, because He who is in you is greater than he who is in the world. (1 John 4:4)

Yet in all these things we are more than conquerors through Him who loved us. (Romans 8:37)

Now thanks be to God who always leads us in triumph in Christ... (2 Corinthians 2:14)

Stand your ground, putting on the sturdy belt of truth and the body armor of God's righteousness. (Ephesians 6:14)(NLT)

The belt is the part of an ancient soldier's armor that held most of the other pieces together. The truth of God's word must be in place first. This truth of Jesus' complete victory over Satan, demons and all evil influence must be revealed to your heart or the rest of the armor is of no use.

The ancient soldier's body armor also included a breastplate. Our spiritual breastplate of righteousness protects the heart. Satan loves to attack you with accusations that God doesn't love you. He will try to injure you with guilt about past failures and mistakes. But remember, your righteousness isn't based on what you can do for yourself. Your righteousness is a gift and is based on what Jesus did for you.

For shoes, put on the peace that comes from the Good News, so that you will be fully prepared. (Ephesians 6:15)(NLT)

The peace of God will protect you from worry, anxiety and fear. Satan would love to distract you from the battle by filling your mind with pictures of all the bad things that could happen to you. This peace must be firmly attached to your mind and spirit just as a warrior's shoes must be firmly attached to fight a battle.

In every battle you will need faith as your shield to stop the fiery arrows aimed at you by Satan. (Ephesians 6:16)(NLT)

You may have imagined the shield of faith to look like a metal trash can lid. The ancient soldier's shield was much more than that. It was large enough for a soldier to crouch behind for protection from flaming arrows and rocks. Faith comes from the word of God (**Romans 10:17**). The shield of faith is put in place by regularly hearing, believing and speaking God's word.

> *Put on salvation as your helmet, and take the sword*
> *of the Spirit, which is the word of God. (Ephesians*
> *6:17)(NLT)*

The helmet protects the mind, Satan's primary battleground. He will attempt to control your mind and emotions. He wants you to be depressed. He wants you to be angry. Salvation frees you from Satan's control. When you have a revelation from God that you can be free from the Devil's influence, you have put on the helmet of salvation.

There is only one offensive weapon described here; the sword of the Spirit. The sword you use to defeat the Devil and all his cohorts is the "word" (Greek – "rhema") of God. The rhema of God is His word personally revealed to you. God's word is like a two-edged sword (**Hebrews 4:12**). One edge is sharpened as God speaks to you through His word. The other edge is sharpened as you speak His word out of your mouth. Jesus used the rhema-word of God to defeat Satan three times in a row in the Garden of Gethsemane. Satan tempted Jesus and He responded with, "It is written…" to put the Devil on the run. You can do the same.

> *Pray at all times and on every occasion in the*
> *power of the Holy Spirit. Stay alert and be persis-*
> *tent in your prayers for all Christians everywhere.*
> *(Ephesians 6:18)(NLT)*

Soldiers put a high premium on being physically fit. They work hard and long to prepare themselves for a time in battle where they will need stamina and strength. Praying regularly with the Holy Spirit's help will strengthen you in your spirit to be able to stand against the attacks of the enemy (**1 Corinthians 14:2,4 & 14-15 & Jude 20**).

VIOLENCE IS REQUIRED

Jesus told us to pray that God's kingdom and His will would be manifested on Earth. He told us to pray that way because we have an adversary who has the opposite agenda. Our adversary, the Devil, wants to STOP God's kingdom and will from being manifested on Earth. If everything that happens on Earth were God's will, we would not have to pray since God would have His way all the time anyway. I know from experience this is not the case.

In this manner, therefore, pray: Our Father in heaven, Hallowed be Your name. Your kingdom come. Your will be done On earth as it is in heaven. (Matthew 6:9-10)

John the Baptist was a forerunner for Jesus. John had been arrested and jailed and was having doubts about whether Jesus was really the Messiah. John sent word to Jesus to ask if He really was the One they had been waiting for. Jesus used the occasion to teach a large crowd about the importance of John's ministry. He also provided a glimpse of the exalted position of all who would be born again because of Jesus. Then Jesus made a statement about the violence required to establish His kingdom on the Earth.

"Assuredly, I say to you, among those born of women there has not risen one greater than John the Baptist; but he who is least in the kingdom of heaven is greater than he. "And from the days of John the Baptist until now the kingdom of heaven suffers violence, and the violent take it by force. (Matthew 11:11-12)

Satan is extremely violent. He wants to steal, kill and destroy. This is why the Scriptures warn us against having anything to do with the works of darkness. Think about the violent actions of people controlled by the Devil described in the Bible. Satan motivated Cain to kill his own brother, Abel. Satan inspired Pharaoh to order the murder of all the male babies born to the Israelites in Egypt. It is easy to gloss over these Scriptures, but think about what really happened. Soldiers came into Jewish houses, took little babies out of their mother's arms and ran their swords through innocent children. After Jesus' first sermon, the crowd wanted to throw Him off a cliff to His death. King Herod, in a drunken stupor, ordered that John the Baptist be beheaded and his severed head brought into the party on a serving platter!

After Satan influenced the two students at Columbine to terrorize and kill in their school, he told them to take their own lives. He continues to motivate religious extremists to become suicide bombers, taking their own lives along with innocent people. The Devil will use you and lie to you in order to accomplish his agenda. When he is through with you, he will throw you away like a piece of trash. He is ruthless and vicious and you will have to be aggressive and violent to stand up to him and drive him out of the circumstances of your life. He won't leave you alone just because you politely ask him.

Jesus gave His disciples a pop quiz one day. He wanted to find out if they really understood who He was. So He asked them a question.

When Jesus came into the region of Caesarea Philippi, He asked His disciples, saying, "Who do men say that I, the Son of Man, am?" So they said, "Some say John the Baptist, some Elijah, and others Jeremiah or one of the prophets." He said to them, "But who do you say that I am?" Simon Peter answered and said, "You are the Christ, the Son of the living God." Jesus answered and said to him, "Blessed are you, Simon Bar-Jonah, for flesh and blood has not revealed this to you, but My Father who is in heaven. "And I also say to you that you are Peter, and on this rock I will build My church, and the gates of Hades shall not prevail against it. (Matthew 16:13-18)

Peter gave the right answer. Jesus told Peter that God had brought that revelation in his heart. Jesus also called Simon (the son of Jonah) by the name of Peter. The Greek word He used for Peter was "Petros" which means "a piece of rock." Then Jesus said He would build His church on a "rock" (Greek word "petra" – a massive rock). The "massive rock" Jesus referred to is the revelation that Jesus is the Christ, the anointed One, and the Son of God. No one can become part of the church of the living God until he has a revelation in his heart of Jesus as the anointed Savior and Son of God. That is the "rock" of revelation on which the church is built.

Jesus said the gates of Hades would not be able to prevail against the church. The "church" consists of all believers, regardless of their denominational label. Remember, if you can control the gate into someone's domain, you can control what happens there. Jesus painted a picture of a church which was to be on the OFFENSIVE, attacking the domain of Satan. Jesus regularly went into Satan's territory and set people free from the Devil's bondage. The church is to be the same way. We shouldn't be hiding behind the church building walls begging people to come in and be saved. We should be going into the Devil's territory with the authority of Jesus' name and taking back what the Devil has stolen!

Imagine a scenario of a small-town bank with a police officer standing in the lobby. A man walks in the bank, puts on a mask, walks up to a teller and says, "Give me all your money." The teller gives him the money, the man calmly walks past the police officer and out of the bank with the stolen money. In a few minutes, the Chief of Police arrives and begins his investigation. He speaks to the teller and then asks the police officer for his version of the story. The officer explains what happened.

"Chief, it was the most amazing thing I have ever seen. This guy walks in the bank and looks right at me. He saw my police badge and my weapon. He went up to the teller and robbed the bank right in front of me. He knew I had the authority to arrest him. He knew I had a weapon which could harm him. But he still robbed the bank. I don't understand it, Chief."

How do you think the Chief would respond? Probably something like this.

"Are you crazy? Just having authority isn't enough. You have to USE IT! You should have pulled out your weapon, walked up to the robber and shouted, "You are under arrest! You will not rob this bank while I am here!"

Unfortunately, many Christians are like this police officer. They don't use the authority Jesus gave them. They stand back and watch the Devil rob them of their money, get their children on drugs and into crime, make them sick, destroy their marriages, etc. They need to take a stand against the Devil. They need to shout at Satan and his demons, "Stop it Devil! You will not get my children on drugs. You demons of drug abuse, in the name of Jesus, I declare my children OFF LIMITS! Devil, stay out of my marriage! Sickness, I command you to go, in the name of Jesus!"

The Devil is violent and aggressive. You can't be passive and hope he will eventually go away and leave you alone. If you want to put him on the run, you have to <u>violently</u> resist him when he tries to gain entrance into your life.

CHAPTER 12

SPEAKING YOUR AUTHORITY

God put the Earth in order by speaking. God's words have great power. He believed what He spoke. What He spoke happened because He believed what He spoke would happen. God spoke the worlds into existence by the authority and power of His words.

> *By faith we understand that the worlds [during the successive ages] were framed (fashioned, put in order, and equipped for their intended purpose) by the word of God, so that what we see was not made out of things which are visible. (Hebrews 11:3)(AMP)*

God created man (mankind – human beings) to be like Him. We can never be God, but we can learn to function similar to the way God functions.

> *So God created man in His own image; in the image of God He created him; male and female He created them. (Genesis 1:27)*

Children learn to act like their parents. They are around them so much they can't help but take on some of the characteristics of their parents. That is why it is so important for parents to set good examples. Our Father God has set a good example. We should endeavor to act like Him. God demonstrated the authority of words. We need to learn to imitate God by using the power of words.

> *Therefore be imitators of God [copy Him and follow His example], as well-beloved children [imitate their father]. (Ephesians 5:1)(AMP)*

Exercising your authority on Earth over Satan and demons is very simple. You speak God's will into existence. God did it. Jesus did it. Every Christian needs to learn to do it. God's will is that you would overcome the attacks of the enemy. God's will is that you would live in His kingdom and resist everything from the kingdom of darkness. You can do this because of the victory Jesus gave you when He shed His blood to free you from the power of sin. Now you can use your words, your testimony, to overcome the Devil. You do it by using the delegated authority God has given you.

> *And they overcame him by the blood of the Lamb and by the word of their testimony... (Revelation 12:11)*

DELEGATED AUTHORITY

Moses had to learn about using delegated authority. God had used Moses to confront Pharaoh over and over about freeing the Israelites. Finally, Pharaoh told Moses and the Hebrew people to leave Egypt. They gladly packed their belongings and left. Then Pharaoh changed his mind. He gathered his armies and pursued Moses and the Israelites. Moses got as far as the shores of the Red Sea. When the armies of Pharaoh got close enough for the Israelites to see them, the Israelites began to cry out to God in prayer. They were afraid. Moses tried to comfort them by telling them God would protect them. But God had another incredible miracle plan. He gave Moses a command to move forward. <u>When God speaks a word of command He also supplies the power to accomplish what He said to do.</u> He told Moses to use his rod to part the Red Sea.

> *Then the L*ORD *said to Moses, "Why are you crying out to me? Tell the people to get moving! Use your shepherd's staff—hold it out over the water, and a path will open up before you through the sea. Then all the people of Israel will walk through on dry ground. (Exodus 14:15-16)(NLT)*

Moses had a choice. He could give up and be defeated by Pharaoh's army. Or he could obey God and use his delegated authority to accomplish a great miracle. Moses chose to use his authority.

> *Then Moses raised his hand over the sea, and the L*ORD *opened up a path through the water with a strong east wind. The wind blew all that night, turning the seabed into dry land. So the people of Israel walked through the sea on dry ground, with walls of water on each side! (Exodus 14:21-22)(NLT)*

What an incredible miracle! This is an awesome example of God's power manifested through man's authority. Moses did not have the <u>power</u> to part the Red Sea. But he had the <u>authority</u> to do it because of what God spoke to him. When Moses obeyed God and exercised his <u>authority</u>, God's <u>power</u> was manifested to accomplish His will. The same principle can be in effect in your life when you understand and use the delegated authority God has given you over Satan and his demons.

REIGNING AS KINGS

Kings have authority. Kings can get things done quickly. They do this because of their authority. Kings issue decrees. When a king wants to eat, he says, "Bring me a meal." If a king wanted his chariot, he said, "Bring me my chariot." When kings speak, things happen. Did you know God wants Christians to rule and reign over the Devil like kings?

> *For if because of one man's trespass (lapse, offense) death reigned through that one, much more surely will those who receive [God's] overflowing grace (unmerited favor) and the free gift of righteousness [putting them into right standing with Himself] <u>reign as kings in life</u> through the one Man Jesus Christ (the Messiah, the Anointed One). (Romans 5:17)(AMP)*

Because of the blood of Jesus, we can serve in the role of a priest and a king. An Old Testament priest went to God on behalf of the people and to the people on behalf of God. We no longer need a priest to go to God on our behalf. Jesus removed the sin from our lives and made it possible for every Christian to go to God directly and serve as his own priest.

> *John, to the seven churches which are in Asia: Grace to you and peace from Him who is and who was and who is to come, and from the seven Spirits who are before His throne, and from Jesus Christ, the faithful witness, the firstborn from the dead, and the <u>ruler over the kings of the earth</u>. To Him who loved us and washed us from our sins in His own blood, and <u>has made us kings and priests</u> to His God and Father, to Him be glory and dominion forever and ever. Amen. (Revelation 1:4-6)*

Jesus gave a revelation to John about the end times. John described the return of Jesus in the book of the Bible we call Revelation.

> *And He has on His robe and on His thigh a name written: KING OF KINGS AND LORD OF LORDS. (Revelation 19:16)*

Jesus is described as the "King of kings." Who are the "kings" Jesus is the "King" of? Those kings are Christians who now serve on the Earth as kings. Jesus has made us kings in that we can reign on this Earth under His delegated authority. It is important to understand that our authority to reign is delegated from God. We can reign as long as we are living under His guidance and direction. We can issue decrees as long as those decrees line up with His will.

ISSUING A DECREE

A number of years ago an incident happened where I had to reign as a king and issue a decree to the Devil. I was living in Alabama at the time and traveling and preaching fulltime. I went up on a weeknight to the church I was attending. I had to deal with some affairs at their Bible School where I was teaching. There were a lot of cars in the parking lot due to a ministry meeting which was already underway. I parked my car at the side of the church and went inside. About an hour later I left to return home. When I went to where I had parked my car, I found an empty parking slot and some broken glass on the pavement. Someone had stolen my car. I immediately called the police.

As I stood in the parking lot and waited for the police to arrive, I began to ponder what had happened. I could have just gone home and told my wife that, "God must have wanted my car stolen because everything happens for a reason." I could have said, "God is trying to teach me to depend on Him more by allowing my car to be stolen." Instead, I evaluated this incident according to God's word. I knew that Satan comes to "steal, kill and destroy." Stealing my car had the potential to cost me money to replace the car. It had the potential to stop my traveling ministry and hinder me from preaching the gospel. This event wasn't part of the "abundant life" Jesus promised me. I realized that this incident was not from God. This was from Satan and people influenced by demons. I was going to have to deal with the "spiritual hosts of wickedness" and not just the flesh and blood bodies of the people involved.

Standing all alone in that parking lot on a chilly winter night, I began to talk to the Devil. I said, "Satan, in the name of Jesus, give me back my car." If anyone had driven by, they may have thought I was crazy since I was talking to someone not visible. But I knew the unseen spirit world was as real as the world I could contact with my senses. I issued a king's decree to the forces of darkness. I said, "You cannot keep my car! It belongs to God. I command you to release my car unharmed, in the name of Jesus."

A police officer arrived in a few minutes and I sat in his car while he took down all the information about the theft. We could hear the normal police chatter on his radio as we talked about what had happened. In a few minutes, we heard a police officer say over the radio he had pulled behind a stolen car in a rough part of town. He said the driver stopped the car, jumped out and ran away. The police officer read the tag number from that car over the radio. And, guess what? It wasn't my car. I continued with my discussion in the church parking lot with the police officer. In a few minutes, we heard some more chatter on the police radio. Apparently, when that stolen car in the rough part of town stopped and the driver bailed out, a car in front of that car did the same thing. The police officer next to me called to ask for the tag number of the second car that was abandoned suddenly. And guess what? It wasn't my car. The police officer told me my car would probably end up wrecked or stripped to sell off as many parts as possible. Then we heard some more on his radio about the two abandoned cars. It seems that a third car was also abandoned. Then we heard that <u>two</u> cars were abandoned in front of the one the police officer originally pulled in behind. The police officer read the tag number of the third car. Guess what? It was my car!

I am grateful for the help of the police department. But I believe it was my decree in the mighty name of Jesus that ultimately caused the people who stole my car to bail out and leave it alone. Remember, the police officer did not pull in behind my car. He was two cars back. Maybe my decree also caused the Devil to give up those other two stolen cars!

GOD'S WILL ON EARTH

God wants His will established on Earth. God will eventually move Heaven to Earth. His will doesn't happen automatically. We have to pray it into being. That is why Jesus told us we should pray for God's kingdom to be established on Earth and for His will to be done.

> *"In this manner, therefore, pray: Our Father in heaven, Hallowed be Your name. Your kingdom come. Your will be done On earth as it is in heaven. (Matthew 6:9-10)*

I have made a number of ministry trips to foreign countries. Even though I was in a foreign country, I was still a United States citizen. I carried a passport that verified I was a U.S. citizen. Your spiritual citizenship changes when you become a Christian. You continue to physically live on this Earth. But your eternal destination will be in Heaven with Jesus. That is why you have a Heavenly passport, signed with the blood of Jesus, which verifies your citizenship is in Heaven.

> *For our citizenship is in heaven, from which we also eagerly wait for the Savior, the Lord Jesus Christ, (Philippians 3:20)*

The United States has ambassadors to represent their interests in other countries. The job of an ambassador is to communicate the opinions of their home country. U.S. ambassadors to other countries are not free to speak their own opinion. They have to check with their superiors in Washington D.C. before they respond to requests for information. They should only speak the policies and will of the United States.

You are an ambassador representing your home country of Heaven. You should only be speaking the will of your superior, Jesus.

> *Now then, we are ambassadors for Christ, as though God were pleading through us: we implore you on Christ's behalf, be reconciled to God. (2 Corinthians 5:20)*

Let's look again at the time when Jesus asked His disciples who they thought He was. Jesus responded by giving Peter the key to establishing God's kingdom on the Earth.

When Jesus came into the region of Caesarea Philippi, He asked His disciples, saying, "Who do men say that I, the Son of Man, am?" So they said, "Some say John the Baptist, some Elijah, and others Jeremiah or one of the prophets." He said to them, "But who do you say that I am?" Simon Peter answered and said, "You are the Christ, the Son of the living God." Jesus answered and said to him, "Blessed are you, Simon Bar-Jonah, for flesh and blood has not revealed this to you, but My Father who is in heaven. "And I also say to you that you are Peter, and on this rock I will build My church, and the gates of Hades shall not prevail against it. "And I will give you the keys of the kingdom of heaven, and whatever you bind on earth will be bound in heaven, and whatever you loose on earth will be loosed in heaven." (Matthew 16:13-19)

The Amplified translation of the Bible gives a more complete description of Jesus' explanation.

I will give you the keys of the kingdom of heaven; and whatever you bind (declare to be improper and unlawful) on earth must be what is already bound in heaven; and whatever you loose (declare lawful) on earth must be what is already loosed in heaven. (Matthew 16:19)(AMP)

The "keys" Jesus gave us is the ability to speak God's will into existence. Jesus said we could command what is available in Heaven to be established here on Earth. He said we could command what is not allowed in Heaven to be removed here on Earth. For example, is health lawful and in free supply in Heaven? Yes, it is. Then you can "loose" or declare health and healing in your life on Earth. Is there sickness in Heaven? No, there is not. Therefore, you can "bind" or declare sickness to leave your body on Earth. Is there fear in Heaven? No. Then you can declare it unlawful in your life on

Earth. Is there peace in Heaven? Yes. Then you can loose peace and declare it lawful in your life on Earth.

So how do you know what you can "bind or declare unlawful" and what you can "loose or declare lawful?" You have to know God's will. To know God's will, you have to know how He thinks. One way God's will is revealed to us is through His word. Many times, His thoughts are different than our thoughts. But He has chosen to reveal His thoughts to us in the form of His word, the Bible.

> *"My thoughts are completely different from yours,"*
> *says the LORD. "And my ways are far beyond*
> *anything you could imagine. For just as the heav-*
> *ens are higher than the earth, so are my ways higher*
> *than your ways and my thoughts higher than your*
> *thoughts. "The rain and snow come down from the*
> *heavens and stay on the ground to water the earth.*
> *They cause the grain to grow, producing seed for the*
> *farmer and bread for the hungry. It is the same with*
> *my word. I send it out, and it always produces fruit.*
> *It will accomplish all I want it to, and it will prosper*
> *everywhere I send it. (Isaiah 55:8-11)(NLT)*

God says His thoughts are higher than our thoughts. But He also says that rain starts out high in the heavens and comes down to the Earth. Then He explains that His thoughts are not kept higher than us but sent down to the Earth in the form of His word.

Another way to determine God's will is by the revelation of the Holy Spirit. Many decisions we have to make are not covered in the Bible - Which house to buy - What job to take - Who to marry. God, by the Holy Spirit living inside the believer, can lead us and communicate specific direction to us.

> *For all who are led by the Spirit of God are children*
> *of God. (Romans 8:14)(NLT)*

Believers have the authority to speak God's will into existence. God's delegated authority brings God's power into play in your life.

God's will is revealed to us by His written word and by the Holy Spirit. We do not have the authority to speak <u>our</u> will into existence unless <u>our</u> will agrees with <u>God's</u> will. For example, Moses wasn't the only person with a rod when Pharaoh was closing in on the Israelites. What if one of the others in the crowd had lifted his rod toward the Red Sea? Would it have parted? No, because <u>God's power only follows His delegated authority</u>. Moses was the only one with the delegated authority to accomplish that miracle. You can't just decree anything you want and expect God to back you up. You can only tap into God's power when you are speaking His will.

> *Who is he who speaks and it comes to pass, if*
> *the Lord has not authorized and commanded it?*
> *(Lamentations 3:37)(AMP)*

But when you know God's will, you can speak words of faith and trust God to cause those words to become reality. The best way to speak in line with God's will is to speak God's word. God has revealed His will in His word. You don't have to go to a psychic to predict your future. You can predict your own future by speaking in line with God's will. For example, I predict that I know the voice of my shepherd, Jesus, and will follow Him only. I predict that God will meet all my needs according to His riches in glory. I predict that I will have the peace of God in the midst of any tribulation. I can speak those things into existence because they are all based on God's word. I know every one of those statements is the will of God because they are the word of God. Remember that Jesus spoke God's word when He was tempted in the wilderness by Satan. The Devil could not stand against the power of God's word.

WORDS OF AUTHORITY

Jesus spoke to demons with the authority of a man without sin. Demons had to obey Jesus' commands.

> *A man possessed by an evil spirit was in the syna-*
> *gogue, and he began shouting, "Why are you both-*

ering us, Jesus of Nazareth? Have you come to destroy us? I know who you are—the Holy One sent from God!" Jesus cut him short. "Be silent! Come out of the man." At that, the evil spirit screamed and threw the man into a convulsion, but then he left him. Amazement gripped the audience, and they began to discuss what had happened. "What sort of new teaching is this?" they asked excitedly. "It has such authority! Even evil spirits obey his orders!" (Mark 1:23-27)(NLT)

Jesus taught His disciples about the power of words. He even spoke to a tree one day.

Now the next day, when they had come out from Bethany, He was hungry. And seeing from afar a fig tree having leaves, He went to see if perhaps He would find something on it. When He came to it, He found nothing but leaves, for it was not the season for figs. In response <u>Jesus said to it</u>, "Let no one eat fruit from you ever again." And His disciples heard it. (Mark 11:12-14)

The next day the result of Jesus speaking to the tree was evident. Jesus took this opportunity to teach His disciples about using their words to activate their faith.

Now in the morning, as they passed by, they saw the fig tree dried up from the roots. And Peter, remembering, said to Him, "Rabbi, look! The fig tree which You cursed has withered away." So Jesus answered and said to them, "Have faith in God. "For assuredly, I say to you, whoever <u>says</u> to this mountain, 'Be removed and be cast into the sea,' and does not doubt in his heart, but believes that those things he <u>says</u> will be done, he will have whatever he <u>says</u>. (Mark 11:20-23)

As you go through life you will encounter obstacles that attempt to keep you from fulfilling God's plan for your life. Many are put there by our enemy, Satan. These obstacles may seem like insurmountable mountains in your path. Jesus said when you encounter these obstacles that seem like mountains, you can speak to them and command them to move. He did not say to ask God to move the mountain for you. Jesus said to use your authority and command that mountain of resistance to move. Notice that Jesus talked about the importance of what you **say** three different times in the same sentence.

Here is another example of how God changes things through the power of words. Abram was a man of great faith. God gave Abram specific instructions and promised He would cause him to become the beginning of a great nation made up of his descendants.

> *Now the* Lord *had said to Abram: "Get out of your country, From your family*
> *And from your father's house, To a land that I will show you. I will make you a great nation; I will bless you And make your name great; And you shall be a blessing. I will bless those who bless you, And I will curse him who curses you;*
> *And in you all the families of the earth shall be blessed." (Genesis 12:1-3)*

Abram was childless and 75 years old when he left his home country of Haran. After several years, Abram began to wonder how God's promises would ever happen. Abram and his wife, Sarai, had been unable to have children. One day Abram said to the Lord that it looked like his servant would have to become his heir because of he and Sarai's inability to conceive a child. God answered with a reminder of His promise.

> *And behold, the word of the* Lord *came to him, saying, "This one shall not be your heir, but one who will come from your own body shall be your heir." Then He brought him outside and said, "Look now toward heaven, and count the stars if*

you are able to number them." And He said to him,
"So shall your descendants be." And he believed in
the LORD, and He accounted it to him for righteous-
ness. (Genesis 15:4-6)

Time continued to pass by. Months turned into years until Abram was 99 and Sarai was 90 and still without a child. Suddenly, God spoke to Abram again.

When Abram was ninety-nine years old, the LORD
appeared to Abram and said to him, "I am Almighty
God; walk before Me and be blameless. "And I will
make My covenant between Me and you, and will
multiply you exceedingly." Then Abram fell on his
face, and God talked with him, saying: "As for Me,
behold, My covenant is with you, and you shall be
a father of many nations. "No longer shall your
name be called Abram, but your name shall be
Abraham; for I have made you a father of many
nations. (Genesis 17:1-5)

God changed Abram's name to Abraham. Why? Abraham means "father of a multitude." God was speaking His faith and helping Abraham to speak his faith, also. Every time Abraham told someone his name, he was saying, "I am the father of a multitude." Whenever God spoke to Abraham, He was calling him the "father of a multitude." In God's eyes, once He spoke His will in faith, it was a done deal. Paul referred to this incident in describing the life of Abraham as an example of great faith.

Therefore it is of faith that it might be according to
grace, so that the promise might be sure to all the
seed, not only to those who are of the law, but also
to those who are of the faith of Abraham, who is the
father of us all (as it is written, "I have made you
a father of many nations") in the presence of Him
whom he believed—God, who gives life to the dead

*and <u>calls those things which do not exist as though</u>
<u>they did</u>; (Romans 4:16-17)*

God spoke things into existence that did not exist until He spoke.
We are supposed to be imitators of our Father. We should speak
God's will into existence. The Devil wants to stop God's will, but
believers can use their faith to defeat the enemy with their words. We
do it because of the delegated authority God has given the believer.

ANGELS

Angels are supernatural beings sent from God to help believers.
They are here to help us.

*And God never said to an angel, as he did to his
Son, "Sit in honor at my right hand until I humble
your enemies, making them a footstool under your
feet." But angels are only servants. They are spirits
sent from God to care for those who will receive
salvation. (Hebrews 1:13-14)(NLT)*

How can you get angels to work on your behalf? Is there a way
to activate angels?

*Bless the LORD, you His angels, Who excel in
strength, who do His word, Heeding the voice of
His word. (Psalm 103:20)*

Angels obey the word of God. This means two things. God can
speak to angels and command them into action. But, believers can
also do something to initiate angelic assistance. Angels heed the
voice of God's word. When they hear God's word spoken in faith,
they jump into action. They stand ready to assist. But you make the
choice whether to activate them or keep them on standby.

You can say things like, "I don't know where we will get the
money to make the next house payment." Your angels will remain on
standby. They are ready to help, but they are hindered because they

can only respond to the voice of God's word. If you refuse to give voice to God's word, you have effectively shut down your angels.

However, you could say something like, "Thank God we have sown bountifully and God is causing our financial seeds to be multiplied back to us." "We have brought our tithes into the storehouse and God is opening up the windows of Heaven and pouring us out a blessing that is more than we can contain." "Thank God all our needs are met according to His riches in Christ Jesus." When you give "voice" to God's word, your angels instantly spring into action. They are on a mission to cause what you said to be manifested in your life.

Daniel was a great Old Testament believer who went on a fast of three weeks to gain understanding from God about a vision he had received.

> *In the third year of Cyrus king of Persia a message was revealed to Daniel, whose name was called Belteshazzar. The message was true, but the appointed time was long; and he understood the message, and had understanding of the vision. In those days I, Daniel, was mourning three full weeks. I ate no pleasant food, no meat or wine came into my mouth, nor did I anoint myself at all, till three whole weeks were fulfilled. (Daniel 10:1-3)*

After three weeks, an angel appeared to Daniel. The angel would go on to explain why it had taken so long to get the answer to him. But first, the angel revealed he had started his journey when Daniel first spoke.

> *Suddenly, a hand touched me, which made me tremble on my knees and on the palms of my hands. And he said to me, "O Daniel, man greatly beloved, understand the words that I speak to you, and stand upright, for I have now been sent to you." While he was speaking this word to me, I stood trembling. Then he said to me, "Do not fear, Daniel, for from*

the first day that you set your heart to understand, and to humble yourself before your God, your words were heard; and __I have come because of your words__. (Daniel 10:10-12)

If Daniel had not spoken, the angel would not have been dispatched. Your words, spoken in prayer, in line with God's will, are important!

God has given you great authority. Use your words wisely and you will consistently overcome all the Devil tries to throw in your path.

CPSIA information can be obtained at www.ICGtesting.com
Printed in the USA
BVOW031110101011

273259BV00001B/280/A